From Buchenwald to Carnegie Hall

From Buchenwald to Carnegie Hall

Marian Filar and Charles Patterson

University Press of Mississippi / Jackson

Willie Morris Books in
Memoir and Biography

Photographs courtesy of Marian Filar
www.upress.state.ms.us

10 09 08 07 06 05 04 03 02 4 3 2 1

Library of Congress Cataloging-in-Publication Data

Filar, Marian, 1917–
    From Buchenwald to Carnegie Hall / Marian Filar and
Charles Patterson.
        p.   cm.
    Includes index.
    ISBN 1-57806-419-8 (cloth : alk. paper)
    1. Filar, Marian, 1917–   2. Pianists—Poland—Biography.
I. Patterson, Charles.   II. Title.

ML417.F43 A3   2002
786.2'092—dc21
[B]   2001026907

British Library Cataloging-in-Publication Data available

*To my dear parents and
other family members murdered
in the Holocaust . . . and to my
sister and brothers who survived*

Contents

Prefatory Note

For a very long time I hesitated to come out with my story, even while I read the experiences of others who had emerged alive from the incredible hell of World War II. Somehow I felt that this was my private life and I was not ready to talk about it. I just kept it inside me all these years. But having retired and being constantly prodded by my friends here and in Europe to tell my story so that it would not be forgotten, I finally decided to give it a try.

My life wasn't ended by the Nazis, although they took much of it away by murdering most of my family. My life went on. I was and am a musician, a teacher, a performer, and a concert artist who has had a long international career. And that life, too, is part of my story.

—*Marian Filar*

Prelude

New Year's Day 1952. Marian Filar waits backstage in Carnegie Hall's green room before playing a concert with Eugene Ormandy and the Philadelphia Orchestra. For the previous three days, he has performed with them in Philadelphia, but this concert in New York is different. Inviting Filar to play the Chopin F Minor Second Concerto, Ormandy said, "This will be the first time in the history of the Philadelphia Orchestra that we have introduced a soloist in New York. Normally, a person has to play himself to pieces giving recitals in New York before we invite him to play with us. We don't *introduce* people."

Filar feels immensely grateful and on the verge of a great breakthrough. He has been in the United States for less than two years, and he is about to make his Carnegie Hall debut. The importance of the occasion makes that special feeling backstage before a performance—part nervousness, part euphoria—all the more intense. He feels that sense of eagerness and anticipation, but he also wonders if everything will go all right. Will he be in control but still able to surrender himself to that higher, stronger force?

The sounds of the audience and the orchestra tuning up are screened out, making the green room eerily silent. He feels buoyed, knowing that out there a group of people is waiting expectantly for him. He can't see or hear them, but he can feel their energy. He wants his playing to transport the audience into that other world of exquisitely beautiful music, into the soul of the composer. He is the medium. He is the artist. He is the performer. All these people have come to see and hear him. His pulse beats firmly. His fingers are chilly, his cheeks warm. The agony of waiting is getting to him—if he doesn't get out on the stage soon, he thinks he will burst.

"Five minutes, Mr. Filar."

He looks in the mirror. Every hair in place. Tie straight. Shirt immaculate. Cuffs where they should be. He adjusts the lapel of his tailcoat—not that he needs to, but it is something to do. He makes sure all the buttons are fastened, his shoes tied. Yes, everything is in place. All is as it should be.

He takes one last look at the face staring back at him. What a long and painful journey it has been. Who would have thought when he arrived on the refugee troop ship, knowing barely a word of English, that in less than two years he would be waiting backstage to play in Carnegie Hall? Eight years earlier, as he stood at attention in his striped black and white uniform in a Nazi concentration camp, listening to a harangue about how he was soon to be killed for being a Jew, who would have imagined that he would ever play again, especially after a guard sliced open his finger and severed the nerve? Who would have thought that the child prodigy who played with the Warsaw Philharmonic when he was twelve and won competition after competition would survive the hell of the Warsaw Ghetto and the Nazi camps? Or that he would carry painful memories buried so deep that forty more years would have to pass before he could even try to put words to them?

"You're on, Mr. Filar."

The sudden rush of adrenaline. The short walk backstage to the wings, to the curtain, and out into the brilliant lights shining on the stage. The burst of applause that greets him as he walks purpose-fully across the polished floor to the gleaming black Steinway con-cert grand. The scent of perfume and aftershave from hundreds of men and women, the sparkle of jewelry in the dimness, the glow of faces whose features he cannot make out, the reassurance that his brothers are somewhere out there in the crowd. The bow to Maestro Ormandy, the adjusting of the black padded piano bench, the lifting of the hands, the nod from the conductor. Music.

Part 1:

Old World

Early Training

I was born in Warsaw, Poland, on December 17, 1917, the youngest of seven children. I grew up living in a large apartment at 18 Gesia Street in a Jewish neighborhood in the northern part of the city, later part of the Warsaw Ghetto. We were a musical family, and there was always lots of singing and music playing at home. My parents were great people who were always encouraging us and joining in on the merrymaking.

Most of our musical interest and talent came from my wonderful mother, who adored music and encouraged us all to play instruments. Although she played the piano only a little bit, she had a special love for music that she passed on to all of us. She once told me that while coming home from school, she regularly went out of her way to pass a private home where a piano was often played. She would stand outside the house and listen for as long as the music continued, forgetting to go home.

My brother Ignaz and my sisters Helen and Lucy played the piano, while my brothers Joel and George played the violin. Although Ignaz never studied a note, he sang beautifully and played totally by ear. He was a great entertainer and the life of the party, and he was always played so that family and guests could sing and dance. My brother Michael did not play an instrument, but he loved music immensely. He was the one who most wanted me to succeed as a pianist, always chasing me to the piano to make sure I practiced.

Since my father's wholesale clothing business was just down the block, at 8 Gesia Street, he came home every day for lunch. He was a very bright man and a good provider, but what I remember most about him was his sense of humor. He was the greatest laugher in the world. I'd say to him, "Dad, I'm going to tickle your foot," and he would start laughing without my touching him. When he laughed, the tears would pour out of his eyes. Later, when I was older, we'd sneak out to the movies together to see Charlie Chaplin or some other comedian. My father always laughed the loudest in the movie house, and I wouldn't be far behind him. He had started out being very strict and stern, but he learned to relax as the family grew.

My musical education began in a most informal way. When I was four years old, I started to sneak in on my sister Helen's piano lessons. I would jump up on a chair behind the piano stool and peek over her shoulder, taking it all in with wide-open eyes and ears. I fell in love with the piano instantly. It made the most glorious sound in the world, the most magnificent I had ever heard. I was hooked. From then on I was married to the piano.

Helen's excellent teacher, an older woman with eyes that were a little crossed, didn't appreciate my interference, but she tolerated my curiosity. One week she showed me a piano key and said, "This is middle C. Now play it." I played it and left knowing where middle C was. The next week I was at the piano before the lesson started and proudly pointed out, "That's C."

"Yes," she said, "and that's a C, and that's a C, and that's a C. The next one is a D, now get out of here." Each week the story repeated itself. The teacher showed me a little more until eventually

I had learned the names of all the keys on the piano. Then every once in a while on my own I would tiptoe in and bang around a little bit with one finger. I wasn't playing much of anything, but the wheels were already starting to turn inside my head.

The next summer, when I was five, my mother took me with her to a beautiful spa in northern Poland called Ciechocinek, where people traditionally went for a rest and a "cure." It was similar to what Bath used to be in England. Visitors drank mineral water from its source in a lovely big park and listened to an excellent symphony orchestra, which played concerts of classical music every afternoon. My mother never missed a single one, and, of course, I was always with her.

When we returned home to Warsaw after six weeks at Ciechocinek, I went straight to our upright piano and picked out with one finger most of the beautiful themes from Mozart, Beethoven, and Tchaikovsky that I had heard at the concerts. As you can imagine, this caused quite a sensation among the family members. So my mother arranged to bring me to see Josef Goldberg, a well-known teacher of gifted children with special musical talent. He was the director of the Moniuszko School of Music, a first-rate school named after a famous Polish composer.

We took the streetcar to the Center City and went to 132 Marszalkowska Street, where Mr. Goldberg lived on the top floor. To try out my musical ear, Mr. Goldberg played a ten-note chord using both hands and asked me to tell him what the notes were. I immediately gave my answer, but my mother, who had seen his hands and the piano keys he had pressed, said, "Oh, that's wrong," believing I was off by a half tone.

"No, it *is* a half tone lower, Mrs. Filar," Mr. Goldberg said. "He's dead right. My piano is badly out of tune. He has perfect pitch."

That news convinced my parents that I should begin musical studies. Since both my sisters and Ignaz already played the piano, my parents decided that I should study the violin like George and

Joel. So they bought me a quarter-sized "baby" violin. It said "Stradivarius" on the inside, but it wasn't.

The first time they handed it to me and I tried to play, I immediately started to cry and make a scene. I hated the thing. I couldn't find the right tone, the right key, the right way to play on pitch. It drove me crazy. You never heard such a noise. That violin wailed and squeaked and screeched so much that it sounded like it was trying to scare all the mice out of the house. It was awful! I carried on and fussed, crying, "I don't wanna, I don't wanna." I made myself so obnoxious that they finally figured it wasn't worth it and switched me to the piano. Then I was happy. Life was all sunshine again. I had already fallen in love with the sound of the piano and that was what I wanted to play—the piano and only the piano. That has never changed.

Because I had such a good ear, Mr. Goldberg took me on as one of his private students, and I studied piano with him from ages six to twelve. When I began, Helen used to take me by the hand to my lessons. Mr. Goldberg had a concert-sized E-Bach—a nine-foot grand—that from my perspective looked about fifty feet long. When we reached the top floor, waiting there would be that enormous piano that made such a big sound! In the beginning, because I was still so small, Mr. Goldberg had special pedals put on his piano to raise them to the level of my feet, which didn't even come close to touching the floor when I sat on the piano bench. I always enjoyed my lessons with him, and our whole family liked him and enjoyed his company. He was a man of good humor, and we were constantly inviting him to our house on the Jewish holidays to be part of the celebration and ritual.

I did so well with my musical studies that at age six I was asked to give a public performance in the large no. 19 classroom at the Warsaw State Conservatory, which was located in the Center City at Okólnik 1, just off Nowy Świat Street. Since I didn't realize how unusual it was to be playing a recital, I wasn't nervous. To me it was no big deal. Besides, all my brothers and sisters played instruments, so I was just doing something that everyone else in my family did, except that I had a recital. You don't learn to get nervous until you're older.

I played that first recital on a Bechstein piano. Years later I read a book by James and Suzanne Pool entitled *Who Financed Hitler: The Secret Funding of Hitler's Rise to Power, 1919–1933* (New York: Dial Press, 1978). I learned for the first time that the Bechsteins, especially Helene Bechstein, were great promoters and financial supporters of Hitler. Helene Bechstein even went to the trouble of teaching the future mass murderer which fork to use when he dined with wealthy people. The book makes me wonder how many concert pianists around the world know of the Bechsteins' support for Hitler and his cause. It would be hard to believe that any decent human being who knew that would want to play a Bechstein piano ever again.

When I was about seven years old, Mr. Goldberg was so pleased with my progress that he decided to show me off to his teacher, the very famous Aleksander Michalowski, one of the all-time great Polish pianists. Michalowski was as good if not a better pianist than Paderewski, who was an artistic god in Poland as well as the prime minister. But because Michalowski never left Poland, he never became as famous as Paderewski. Michalowski, however, was the true dean of Polish pianists and a great exponent of Chopin's music. When you mentioned Michalowski's name, everyone took his hat off.

When I met him, Michalowski was a very old man, half blind and feeble. I played for him, but I was too young to appreciate the honor. I'm embarrassed to admit that I was more impressed with his French poodle and spent the time under his piano playing with the dog rather than trying to talk with him. What I wouldn't give now to talk to him about music!

I also studied a little with Professor Jerzy Zurawlew of the Chopin Music School. Professor Zurawlew was a remarkable man. He was responsible for starting Poland's International Chopin Competition, one of the world's most prestigious piano competitions. He got the idea in a very funny way. Next to the Conservatory of Music was a big circus building where everyone used to go. As a kid, I went there often and loved every act, especially the clowns and the trapeze artists. There was always quite a crowd. One Saturday Professor Zurawlew was coming out of the Conservatory when he saw a line of people that stretched all the way down the block, a much longer line than usual. He wondered what everyone was waiting for, so he asked someone and found out that the circus was a having a special boxing match. He asked himself, what is it about a boxing match that attracts all these people? He decided that it was the competition, the desire to see who was best, who was going to win. So he thought, "Why can't we take these people away from the circus and bring them to the Conservatory? If everyone likes competitions so much, why not have a competition of music instead?" That was the idea behind Poland's great International Chopin Competition, which began in 1927.

Although I don't remember much about it, I am proud to say that when I was ten I played a mutual recital at the Warsaw State Conservatory with my contemporary, the great violinist Henryk Szeryng. How wonderful that fifty-one years later, after our worlds had collapsed around us, we were able to come together again to teach a master class.

In 1931, when I was still only twelve, I took a big step forward in my career as a pianist and a performer. I auditioned for the Warsaw Philharmonic Orchestra, playing the complete Mozart D Minor Piano Concerto, K.466, for the Philharmonic's conductor, Walerian Bierdjajew. He was so impressed he immediately engaged me to perform the same piece as a soloist with the orchestra. I played, and my performance received excellent reviews. Suddenly I was famous, a celebrity, a hero among my friends!

My parents were delighted. One afternoon soon after the performance I came home from school to find that our faithful old upright was gone—vanished! To my astonishment, a brand-new

five-foot, seven-inch grand piano by Kerntopf, a very good manufac-
turer, stood in its place. It was just waiting there—for me! My parents had never said a word. Suddenly I had a beautiful new piano
and one of the most wonderful surprises of my life.

As a result of my first performance with the Warsaw Philharmonic, I was selected to play the Mozart concerto again a few
months later, this time with the Philharmonic under the baton of
conductor and cellist Kazimierz Wilkomirski. For my encore at the
performance, I played Chopin's Nocturne in E-flat Major, Op. 9,
No. 2. Even at that early age I had an affinity for Chopin, in my
opinion the greatest piano composer of all time. Again, the reviews
were wonderful, and everyone was impressed.

Shortly afterward my parents decided I needed a new teacher.
Mr. Goldberg wanted me to work next on Beethoven's First Piano
Concerto, which was a big mistake. It was too big a step to try to
take without first mastering the fundamentals. Even my mother
knew it was wrong. Mr. Goldberg was just relying on my ear, so he
wasn't working on any of the basics with me. He never mentioned
anything about chords, arpeggios, scales—the techniques that are
the underpinnings of any great technique. So now after my success
with the Philharmonic, he wanted me to learn this very difficult
concerto. It was time to leave.

It so happened that Alfred Hoehn, a great German pianist who
had won the first Anton Rubinstein Piano Competition in Moscow
and who was the director of the Frankfurt Conservatory of Music,
was in Warsaw in preparation for his upcoming performance with
the Philharmonic. He attended my second performance of the Mozart concerto to check out the kid all of Warsaw was talking about.
Afterward, my mother brought me to meet him. Since she had
taken me away from Professor Goldberg, she wasn't sure where to
turn and thought that Mr. Hoehn could offer some advice. He was
very complimentary about me, and, much to our surprise, he offered
to take me to Germany to study with him. He had children my age

with whom I could go to school, so I would have friends while I studied piano.

"When he comes back to you at twenty-one," he told my mother, "he'll be completely trained and ready as a concert pianist. But there is a problem in Germany right now with the Hitlerites. I'm sure it will blow over in a few months, but, until it does, why doesn't he study at the Conservatory here? Then he can come to me when this Hitler business settles down. Each time I visit Warsaw, I'll stop by to monitor his progress."

He recommended that I study with Professor Zbigniew Drze-wiecki, the most admired piano teacher in Poland as well as a distinguished concert pianist who played throughout Europe. He was president of the Chopin Society and of Poland's International Chopin Competition. Professor Drzewiecki was a great man and the leading musician in the country, and he demanded 100 percent all the time.

So the next thing I knew, I was auditioning for Professor Drze-wiecki, and he accepted me for private study during July and August in preparation for the September entrance exam to the Warsaw Conservatory of Music.

That summer of study with Professor Drzewiecki was not the happiest period of my life, to put it mildly. Today I reverently keep his photograph above my piano, but then he was bigger than life and was stern and very intimidating. There was no nonsense about him. When he gave you a look of disapproval, you turned to ice. When he yelled, you shook. He scared me half to death. I remember him always with a cigarette, which he kept between his third and fourth fingers. He was a very, very great man, and it was an honor to be his student, but it wasn't easy. For one thing, he shouted at me at the top of his lungs. And *what* he shouted made it worse.

Here I was, almost a folk hero. Stories about me were appearing in all the newspapers: Marian Filar, who had soloed with the Warsaw Symphony at age twelve; Marian Filar, the prodigy, the new musical sensation, the young genius! And here Professor Drzewiecki was yelling at me! And not very politely. How dare he? I didn't like it at all.

But I have to admit, I did set myself up for it. At our unforgettable first meeting when he asked me what I played, I foolishly but inno-cently enough said, "A concerto." He said that he didn't want to hear it again, that he had been at the concert. Then there was a very long silence, the calm before the storm.

"Do you play scales?" he asked.

"No."

"Do you play arpeggios?"

"No."

"Do you play Czerny études?"

"No."

"Do you play Bach?"

"No."

He exploded, "Then you don't know anything!"

And when Professor Drzewiecki shouted, you wanted to take cover. He was famous for his yelling. On one occasion, my mother was supposed to meet me after my lesson, but she didn't show up, so I had to go home alone. When I got there, I was surprised to find her at home.

"Mother, why didn't you meet me at Professor Drzewiecki's as you said you would?"

"I was there. I was at the door, just about to ring his bell, but when I heard such shouting inside, I got scared and turned around and went home!"

And she had only been *outside* the door! She had no idea what it was like to be in the line of fire!

I was miserable and cried a lot during those two months because I thought of myself as what the newspapers were saying I was—a great young pianist. But I hadn't developed the patience and disci-pline to work on such basics as hand position, wrist position, arm weight, scales, chords, arpeggios, and so on. And what was worse, I didn't know how much I needed to master those things. Thank

God, Professor Drzewiecki scared the hell out of me and forced me to learn them.

At our first lesson he said, "All right, show me your hand position." I did, but my fingers weren't correct. "No, like this," and he shaped my fingers so they were more rounded. "Now, show me your hand position." I did. The fingers were still not right. One in particular wasn't rounded enough.

"No!" he shouted. He grabbed my tiny recalcitrant finger and slammed it into the keyboard. "Like this!"

Ouch! I had to look at my finger to see if all of it was still there!

"Forget about concertos and concerts," he shouted. "You don't even know how the fingers should be placed on the keyboard!" I wanted to hide under the piano. But, in my own defense, how was I supposed to know? No one had ever taught me about hand positions. The truth is, I didn't really know anything about music. I had simply been relying on my ear and not working on the basics. That was all to change.

Even though I eventually came to appreciate Professor Drzewiecki's greatness, that summer with him was pure hell—like Marine boot camp. My early, naive dislike of him later turned into admiration and appreciation for a wonderful teacher, and later still, I came to look upon him as my second father. He was one of the courageous ones who risked his life to help me survive the Holocaust.

Conservatory Days

In September 1932, after two exhausting and unforgettable months of private lessons with Professor Drzewiecki, I sat for my examination to enter the State Conservatory of Music. Professor Drzewiecki prepared the program that I played in front of the musical jury at the Conservatory. When I passed and was accepted into the fourth year of the nine-year program, I was on top of the world! Not only had I been accepted into the fourth year right off the bat, but I had also already played with the Warsaw Philharmonic—a full concerto, not just a kiddie concert! I thought I was the greatest pianist in the universe.

However, my high spirits faded during my first days at the Conservatory, as I walked around and listened outside the practice studios. These kids were good, very good. This was not funny! It was obvious that I was going to have to work hard to keep up. My ego and competitive spirit were immediately engaged by the challenges presented by this great school. Not only did the top talents of Poland vie to attend, but many of the top talents from the rest of Europe were there as well. Chopin, Paderewski, and Arthur Rubinstein had studied there. I decided I'd better sit down at the piano and really start working, which is what I did. I buckled down, and in my first year I got straight A's and did two years worth of study, so I moved directly into the program's sixth year.

There was a light, reassuring moment at the beginning. One of my first days at the Conservatory, a man named Joseph, a caretaker who used to open the pianos, looked at me closely and said, "I remember you! I opened a piano for you when you were just a *stinker* and had bangs and short pants! You played your first recital here." It was nice to be remembered among so many.

Since my Conservatory studies were in addition to my regular schoolwork, things started getting hectic. I was going to school Tuesday through Sunday at a gymnasium (secondary school that prepares students for university) and then attended the Conservatory after my regular classes every day except Sunday. My parents decided it was too much and found another private gymnasium, one of the best in the city, that had Sunday off. Having neither school nor Conservatory on Sunday gave me a little more time to breathe. My mother worried about me running around too much and always catching colds, so she would slip me a sandwich in the afternoon. "You need strength," she would say, "this is good for you. Eat it, but don't tell your father." Why not? Because it was a ham sandwich!

I grew musically by leaps and bounds. I took classes in harmony (two levels), music theory, solfeggio (sight singing, or reading music by singing it), and basic musical theory—reading and analyzing musical forms. The Conservatory had three courses of three years each—low, medium, and high—for a total of nine years of study. After I entered at the fourth-year level and then passed straight into the sixth, I spent the last three years in the Conservatory's final phase.

I continued my studies with Professor Drzewiecki by taking lessons with him at the Conservatory twice a week, and eventually I became one of his favorite students. The students used to compete to run errands for him, and I always seemed to be the one who ended up bringing him his cigarettes, although that didn't mean he made it any easier on me.

In 1937, 1938, and 1939—the seventh, eighth, and ninth years of my program of studies—I won first prize in the piano competition arranged by the Ministry of Culture. As a consequence, I was placed on scholarship, and the ministry sent me a check for fifty zlotys each month. Scholarships to the Conservatory were based on talent, not financial need. I never knew how much my tuition cost my parents. Since it was a state conservatory, it probably wasn't too expensive. We were fairly well off, but it was still a good feeling to know that my dad didn't have to pay for my musical education anymore. I also never knew how much my father paid Mr. Goldberg—that was considered none of my business. My parents kept us out of the financial side of things.

As soon as I started getting the fifty zlotys each month, I no longer had to take money from my dad. He had been giving me an allowance of twelve zlotys a month, but now I was getting that much every week, a lot of extra money for a kid. I walked around with full pockets. I could afford to buy books and music and lunch for my friends. I was a capitalist!

The Conservatory had its own beautiful, large recital hall with a magnificent balcony. Guest artists of the Warsaw Philharmonic played recitals there often, so as students we heard all the great musicians of the day. For me the concerts were always free—even the ones that weren't supposed to be.

One of my group of friends, Stas Jarzembski, was the son of a professor of violin at the Conservatory. Since he could get hold of keys and had access to the service entrance, we used to sneak up the stairs and head towards the big no. 19 classroom where I had played my first concert. It was on the second floor, which was the same floor the recital hall was on. The classroom had a door that connected to the back entrance of the recital hall. All of us, including the girls, would sneak up to the classroom and enter the recital hall through the small hallway, bypassing the main entrance and the ticket takers. Once we got inside the recital hall, we would scatter to the vacant seats. The manager was always complaining that he was going broke from the free seats the students grabbed. "Those kids are going to ruin me!" he would say. The more he carried on, the more we laughed.

I also got in for free because of Professor Drzewiecki, who was a music critic and a terrific writer as well as a professor. When he had conflicting events to go to, he would give me his *passepartout*, reviewer's pass, so I could go into the recital hall for nothing and get a great seat. I was his last student of the day, so he would say, "I can't go to the recital tonight. Listen to it for me, and tomorrow tell me how it was." When I used the pass, the manager would get all red and flustered. "Couldn't you at least give me the tax on the ticket?" he would say. "But then I'd have to give you my streetcar fare, and I live such a long way out," I would answer. "You wouldn't want me walking all that way home so late at night, would you? It'll take me an hour and a half. Here, look in my wallet! I don't have anything except my fare. My mother would be so worried about me."

I was a musician, but that doesn't mean I wasn't athletic or that I spent all my time indoors. With my older brothers at home to wrestle with and have pillow fights with and compete with, I became good at games and sports. I rode a bicycle, swam, and played soccer. I also became a scout leader and had a troop of ten boys under my command. One summer I worked on a farm, harvesting honey from beehives. That summer I remember thinking as I listened to the Polish women singing mazurkas in the fields, "I'm not old enough to play Chopin's mazurkas yet. I need time to understand them."

By going to the Conservatory recitals and to the Warsaw Philharmonic, we got to hear all the famous artists of the day. After I heard Rachmaninoff in person, I got sick, but it was worth it. I had to stand in a line about three blocks long to get a ticket, and it was raining buckets. I didn't have an umbrella, so I got soaked to the skin. I listened to the concert looking like a wet dog and then was in bed for a week, but it was an absolutely fantastic experience. Once I heard Josef Hofmann. His first concert at the Philharmonic wasn't sold out because nobody knew who he was. Then he played the Chopin E Minor Concerto, and we all fell out of our chairs. That same week he played a recital at the Conservatory where he played the Chopin Minute Waltz in double thirds, and you heard every note. He was amazing.

I also heard the great German pianist Walter Gieseking, who would later play such a big part in my life, and Wilhelm Backhaus, Alfred Hoehn, Isidor Philip, Wanda Landowska, and Arthur Rubinstein—you name them, I heard them. We never missed anyone. It was part of our education. And that's why at the end of the year all of us at the Conservatory were easily able to map out our program of study for the following year. Professor Drzewiecki would call us by name, and we would come up to the front of the class. He would ask, "What do you want to play next year?" That was the way it worked. Music wasn't just assigned, although you had to start with Bach. We'd say, "I'd like to play such and such," and he'd say, "That piece is all right," or "No, that's too complicated, but this other one is okay for you, start with that and then we'll see."

He questioned each one of us. "What kind of études would you like to play?" he might ask. "I'd like to play Chopin études." "Okay, you're ready for them. You can take this one and that one. I'll give you two."

"I want to play a sonata," someone might say. "Whose do you want to play, Mozart's or Beethoven's?" "Mozart." "Look at K. such and such."

"I want to play some Brahms," another might say. "Fine. Look at this and this. What Chopin do you want to play?"

Many times when we selected a piece to work on, we had heard it performed so often we almost knew it from memory. Today, students have recordings of all kinds that we didn't dream of. Of course,

78 rpm recordings were beginning to be available, but they cost a fortune, and no one could afford them. Besides, who had anything to play them on? Nobody. Instead, we heard the music live, which was inspiring and much better.

Old Warsaw—the Warsaw that World War II destroyed—was a truly beautiful city, filled with churches, wonderful palaces built during the Middle Ages, and many exotic-looking buildings. The oldest part of Warsaw, called the Old City, was on the Vistula River, which divides Warsaw. The center and heart of the city was a market square dating from the late thirteenth century and surrounded by incredible houses from the fourteenth and fifteenth centuries. Throughout the city were spacious parks, playgrounds, fine libraries, galleries, the University of Warsaw and other schools, theaters for concerts and plays, and a beautiful opera house—one of the largest in the world—plus the presidential palace and its wonderful gardens. When we toured the palace as teenagers, we had to wear special straw shoes so that we wouldn't scratch the magnificent floors. Today Warsaw looks nothing like it once did because 85 percent of the city was destroyed in the war. People can't begin to imagine what Old Warsaw was like.

For me personally, it was a truly wonderful place to live. I had a great time with my family, which included grandparents and lots of cousins, and school friends. It is especially interesting to me now that I am an American citizen to recall that there was only one black man in the entire city, and he worked for the Plutos chocolate company, a very famous firm. All the kids called him Sam. He must have been about seven feet tall and wore a beautiful uniform as he drove around Warsaw in one of the company's trucks. Between one and two o'clock he would make it a point to stop at different schools to give out samples of chocolate. You would see him with two hundred or more kids clustered around him. We were all crazy about Sam and loved him like mad.

Our teachers were wonderful, fantastic, highly educated people. The schools themselves were modest buildings, not like today's large, modern complexes with all the facilities, a huge gym, and thousands of students. We received a lot of attention because there were only about twenty-five or thirty boys in each grade. Our gymnasium had eight grades, or classes, with the one before the first called the entrance class. There were separate schools for boys and girls, but before graduation the boys' and girls' schools got together for a big dance with an orchestra.

For me the very best part about growing up in Warsaw was the tremendous amount of music played in the city, and it was an activity that everyone attended and loved. The Polish Ministry of Culture organized concerts and competitions of all types. Since Warsaw was the country's capital, it was on the main European concert circuit, and everyone who was anyone came through. It was a sophisticated, cosmopolitan city, and audiences expected to hear the best artists. I remember when I went to the opera house for the first time to see *Carmen*, the singer was so bad that when she committed suicide somebody yelled from the gallery, "Don't bother to get up. You were terrible!"

The Philharmonic was a magnificent hall that seated about 2,500, and it was always sold out. The orchestra played three concerts a week, and the Friday night concert was broadcast throughout Europe. There were two concerts every Sunday afternoon, one at noon and one at three. I performed at both of the Sunday concerts, which were broadcast all over the Warsaw area. I remember getting my first radio. I was in bed with a cold, and my father brought me a huge radio, a big box of a thing by Philips with which you could listen to all of Europe. It was fantastic! My uncle, who had a button factory outside of Warsaw and was a very rich man, had already started to manufacture radios named Filaret. They contained a crystal, so when you put a pair of little earphones on, there was a detector with a needle to probe the crystal to get better reception. I listened to the concerts of the Warsaw Philharmonic and the other orchestras of Europe. I also heard seven live recitals a week at the Conservatory of Music.

I continued to study at the Conservatory even after a number of my friends graduated, so the question arose—if I was such a big shot, winning competitions, getting straight A's, and able to pass two years in one, why didn't I take my final exams and start my career? Even the rector of the Conservatory, Professor Eugene Morawski, wanted to know.

One day he called me into his office for a private talk. "I believe in you, Marian," he said. "You have a great career ahead of you. What are you waiting for?"

"I *want* to take my exams, Rector Morawski, but Professor Drzewiecki won't give them to me. Each time I ask him about them, he avoids the subject. I walk him to his streetcar, but when I ask him about taking my exams, he runs away. 'Oh, there's the number 18! That's my streetcar!' And he's gone!"

"Then corner him. Ask him point-blank."

So that's what I did. The next time I saw him I asked about the exams. "Do you want to know the truth?" he asked. "Marian, because you are Jewish, the doors in Poland are closed to you. You know I didn't close them, and you know very well that I'd open them if I could."

"Yes, Professor, I know that."

"I talked to your parents behind your back and asked them to send you abroad, but your father said that with his two daughters preparing to get married, he couldn't afford the expense at this time. If you graduate now, what are you going to do? There will be no work for you in Poland, no suitable places where you can perform and grow. Instead, you will deteriorate. By not graduating, you remain in the Conservatory, continue to study with me, and have an obligation to practice and learn new repertoire. For the time being, I think it's best. We will have to see what happens."

Although my life was happily filled with my music and friends, I slowly began to be aware of the dark clouds on the horizon. Much of what I learned I found out from my father. He told me that once he had wanted to be a lawyer and had passed the required exams, but the law school didn't accept him because he was a Jew. In those days, Warsaw University divided courses into *numerus clausus* and *numerus nullus*. *Numerus nullus* meant courses in which no Jews were allowed; Jews were allowed in *numerus clausus* courses, but only up to a certain percentage. So there was already official anti-Semitism in Poland when my father was a young man, and it only got worse as the influence of Nazi Germany grew.

Instead of becoming a lawyer, my father became a businessman and did quite well. His wholesale clothing business employed ten or twelve people. After my brother Michael finished school, he helped my father run his business. Michael was very special, in many ways the heart and soul of the family. My dad had a hot temper, so when he got mad at clients and threw them out, it was Michael who made peace. Eventually Michael managed the day-to-day part of the business as my father got older. Since my father's business responsibilities sometimes took him to other European countries, he told us about the rising tide of anti-Semitism in Europe.

Although I was fairly insulated from the problem myself, I do remember a couple of incidents. I often played for guests at the Conservatory and elsewhere, usually at the request of Professor Drzewiecki. Once I played the Brzezinski Variations at the Steinway store for the great pianist Ignaz Friedman, who was friends with Professor Drzewiecki. Another time when I was playing the piano at the Conservatory for Professor Drzewiecki and a former student, a well-known pianist who had won the International Vienna Competition, I heard him say to my professor, "It's too bad he's Jewish." I didn't know what he meant by that or what effect my being Jewish would have on my life.

Another incident happened in 1938 after I won my second Ministry of Culture piano competition. An official from the Ministry of Finance's Department of Income Tax showed up at my dad's place of business with a demand that he pay an "income tax" of one hundred thousand zlotys—not a tax on one hundred thousand zlotys, but one hundred thousand zlotys itself, a huge amount.

About a week later, with me in tow, my father confronted the official in his office. "This is my son," he said and showed him some newspaper stories about me. "He's won the Ministry of Culture's piano competition two years in a row. The Ministry of Culture thinks so highly of him, they gave him a scholarship to the Conservatory and pay him fifty zlotys a month while he studies. Someday, the country might be proud that he is a son of Poland. Now tell me, why are you trying to ruin me and my family? Show me where I've cheated. Prove something is owed, and I'll gladly pay it. Otherwise, tell me, why are you doing this?"

There was a pause.

"Mr. Filar," said the official, "if you don't like it here, why don't you go to Palestine?"

My father swallowed what he wanted to say, and we left the office. He hired a lawyer to protest the tax and never paid it.

Although the tax incident illustrates the increasingly open and official anti-Semitism in Poland, I don't think it reflected the attitude of all Polish people. How could I? Poles saved my life and the lives of many other Jews during the war. Prejudice comes in many forms—anti-Jew, anti-Pole, anti-German—and they're all equally ignorant.

My wise and beautiful mother saw Hitler coming and did something about it, thank God. I remember her saying, "One of my kids has to get out of Poland so we'll have a place to lay our heads if we have to run." The "kid" turned out to be my brother George, who went to Palestine in 1935 at age twenty-five. Fortunately, he took with him copies of most of our family photos and documents. Almost all the originals were later destroyed when our apartment burned during the bombing of Warsaw in 1939. I would have had no photos of my family at all if it had not been for George and for my mother's foresight.

George was quite a guy, and everyone liked and admired him. Later he became a folk hero in Israel, but he was a hero to me long before he left Poland. One day in Warsaw he was walking down the street in a Jewish neighborhood—there was no ghetto then—and it was raining heavily, buckets of water pouring down. In front of George was a big tall man and in front of him was an old Jewish woman with a basket of bagels she was selling. She had covered them to protect them from the rain and was walking slowly because she was old. When the big guy saw his streetcar coming, he just shoved the old woman out of his way. She fell and landed on her face in the gutter. All her bagels rolled out of the basket and were ruined. She sat on the pavement and cried, but the big guy paid no attention.

George couldn't believe it. He caught up with the guy from behind, tapped him on the shoulder, and when he turned around, he punched him in the face and knocked out a few of his teeth. The guy went down, and that was it. When he came to, he pulled out his gun and started shooting. He was a police commissioner from another district. A few hours later, a cop came to our door. I don't know how they found out who was responsible, but they did. When George appeared, he was offered greetings from our local police commissioner, who wanted to know if he could buy George a drink. When the two met, the commissioner told George that he had done him a big favor. He personally hated that other guy and had been wanting to hit him for a long time. He shook George's hand and told him to get out of town for a few days until things cooled down, which he did.

Part 2:

Fires of War

War Comes to Warsaw

World War II began on Friday morning, September 1, 1939, with the German invasion of Poland. On Thursday night people were at home eating their dinners. There was still good food, and war was still only a fear. But from Thursday to Friday the world changed. About 5:30 in the morning we began hearing explosions in the skies over Warsaw. I got up and went to my father, who was standing at his bedroom window. I expected to see German planes, but all I saw was little puffs of white clouds in the distant sky, reassuring but harmless evidence of exploding Polish antiaircraft shells.

At first we didn't see any German planes because they flew as high as possible until they could find out what kind of an antiaircraft defense Poland had. Then, when they came down lower, we saw them in their formations. The president of Poland read an announcement over the radio saying that the Germans had treacherously attacked us and we were now at war. It was official.

As we watched the German planes fly in, my father said to me,

"I survived the last war, but I'm not so sure I'll survive this one."
He was right. Two and a half years later, the Nazis murdered him.

The German planes dropped five-hundred–pound bombs on us,
followed by incendiaries. When the bombing started, we took cover
in our building's basement. I will never forget the drone of the German Stuka planes as they came closer and dropped their bombs and
how we waited for the explosion. I didn't know I could hold my
breath so long or that time could stand still like that.

When the bombing stopped, I ran outside, spitting dust, not
knowing what I would see, and unprepared for what I would find.
The apartment building next door received a direct hit, instantly
killing about eighty people. The building now had a grotesque new
shape, half of it blown away, half of it still standing. The section of
its roof still remaining was in flames, but the stairwell, which we
would have used to get to the roof to fight the fire, had collapsed. A
woman, black with dust and grime, sat in the frame of a second-
floor window, screaming for help, her legs dangling outside.

Since the stairs under her had been bombed away, the only way
I could reach her was by scrambling up the steep pile of bricks
formed by the collapsed parts of the building. As I was making my
way up the pile, I felt a hand reach out from under the bricks and
grab at my foot. I heard a faint "Help! Help!" sound, but I couldn't
tell if it was a man or a woman. A woman, I guessed, but I couldn't
be sure. I stopped and tried to dig the bricks away, but for every
brick I pulled away, more bricks came tumbling down. Meanwhile,
our apartment building had caught on fire, and I was needed there.
I couldn't do a damn thing to help the buried person. All I could
do was whisper, "I'm sorry, but it's impossible."

I left the buried person and continued to climb up the bricks to
the woman at the window. I managed to reach her and carry her
down. The superintendent's door was open, so I brought her into
his apartment. She was now unconscious, and I filled a container
with water and splashed it on her face. She woke up with a start

and began yelling at me, "Why are you throwing water on me? I have a cold!"

I couldn't help laughing at the absurdity of the situation. "Lady," I said, "I just saved your life! How was I supposed to know you have a cold?" When I was convinced she was all right, I rushed back to our apartment building to help fight the fire. When I arrived, I was horrified to see that my piano and all my music had caught fire. All I could save was an armful of my sister Helen's clothes, which were hanging neatly in a closet. I grabbed as many as I could and threw them out the window to my father, who was standing below. Almost everything else went up in flames. There had been no time to save anything except essentials—clothing to cover our backs.

Buildings up and down the street were on fire, so things were chaotic. When my mother didn't see my father for a while, she got worried and began asking, "Has anyone seen my husband?" "Oh, yeah," someone said, "he's down the street." He was on the top of a seven-story building, directing a group of younger men he had rounded up to fight a fire.

The woman trapped under the bricks was heavy on my conscience until I learned a few days later that some of her relatives arrived after I left and were able to dig her out of the rubble. She was injured but alive, thank God. So that took the heavy stone off my heart.

The Poles were no match for Hitler's army. They could not stop the onslaught of German tanks. All we could do to defend ourselves as the Germans approached Warsaw was dig trenches. The students at the Conservatory all pitched in, and we dug trenches around the building. Professor Drzewiecki asked me if I could get him a shovel so he could do his part. There wasn't a shovel to be had anywhere in Warsaw, but I had an uncle in the hardware business, so I managed to get a couple of shovels from him. But when I brought them back on the streetcar, everybody wanted one. People offered me all sorts of money. When I said no, they started getting nasty: "What do you need *two* shovels for?" I said, "They're not for me, they belong to somebody else." I was glad to get off that streetcar before things got out of hand!

When I reached the Conservatory and handed Professor Drzewiecki a shovel, he dug up about five ounces of earth and then said, "I'm tired, I have to rest!" He never picked up the shovel again! Professor Drzewiecki was an older man and was not used to this kind of work, and it certainly wasn't good for any pianist to be shoveling. But we students had little choice, so we worked hard, regardless of our hands. But it was all to no avail.

The Conservatory was such a beautiful place, but, like so much of Warsaw, German bombing totally destroyed it. The old Philharmonic, another beautiful building full of memories, was also destroyed early in the war. The Red Cross used it as a hospital for the wounded and painted a red cross on the roof, but the Germans bombed it anyway. It was a disgusting thing to do. They wanted to destroy everything, especially anything that had meaning for the people. And they did.

During the weeks before the German occupation of Warsaw, the planes and the bombings kept everyone on edge. I remember late one afternoon coming home from a friend's house when I noticed a flock of migrating geese, maybe fifty or so of them flying very high in the sky in their V-shaped formation. People on the street started to point up and run for cover. "German airplanes!" they screamed, "German airplanes!" I pointed at them and said, "Hey, they're moving their wings. Planes don't flap their wings, you dopes. It's a flock of birds!" But the city was in a panic because there had already been so much death and destruction.

As soon as it was clear after a bombing raid, we would rush outside to try to help, and help was always needed. After one particularly bad raid, I saw the synagogue across the street on fire. I was a young kid with more guts than sense, so I ran inside it and saved two Torahs. When I came out with one in each arm, an older man said, "Here, I'll take one." I said, "Do your own good deed!"

Before the war I had expected to serve in the Polish army. I passed my physical and was listed as category A. As a member of the educated class, normally I would automatically have been assigned to officers' school. It was a rule that if you finished the gymnasium, you went to officers' school. However, they didn't allow Jews to be officers, although they didn't openly say that as official policy. So, I was never called up to serve in spite of the fact that there was an urgent mobilization underway. The army dropped me from consideration—"deferred" they called it—and gave me some feeble excuse, I don't even remember now what it was. It was a disgusting joke! And so obvious.

I felt deeply hurt by the rejection, especially since the authorities were calling people up in the middle of the night, getting them out of bed, hustling them off. That's how desperate they were for soldiers. They were even drafting *Volksdeutsch,* people of mixed Polish-German ancestry who had lived in Poland for a long time and were citizens. As it turned out, many of these *Volksdeutsch* were helping the Germans by signaling the bombers at night. Not far from where we lived—about a ten- to fifteen-minute drive—was a big cemetery where they caught one traitor in an open grave signaling with a flashlight. Those people they took.

Another traitor, a Polish captain, was even worse. He was a member of the Elks, a Polish Underground group of air bombers that used a secret airfield near the city of Kielce. About three o'clock one morning he got in an airplane and secretly took off. He came back about six, leading a squadron of German bombers, which bombed the airfield to smithereens and then bombed the hell out of the city. Those they took, while they gave me a deferment "to next year." Next year Poland didn't exist. And I used to be such a Polish patriot before the war. I loved my country—you have no idea.

In less than a month the German troops were at the gates of Warsaw. As they came closer to the city, the mayor of Warsaw, Stefan Starzynski, ordered all young people who could carry arms to leave and go east, where we were supposed to form an army to fight the Germans. I was twenty-one, so I began preparing to leave, along with my brother Michael, who was thirty-five, my sister Lucy, twenty-eight, and her husband, Ben, who was twenty-nine. Ben and Lucy had just been married.

On October 1, 1939, my father and I stood on Wolska Street watching the Germans march into Warsaw. They came in from the west, a formidable force, singing as they marched, all rigidly goose-stepping like a machine, all staring straight ahead. I had heard them coming from quite a way off, singing some German song I didn't know but singing it pretty well. I said to my father, "Gee, Dad, listen to that. You can hear where Beethoven's music comes from." My father looked at me and shook his head. "They're coming here to kill us, and you hear Beethoven!"

On October 6 or 7 those of us leaving the city headed off. By October 12 we crossed the Bug River and reached Bialystok in eastern Poland. During the journey we had to constantly run and hide from Luftwaffe pilots, who seemed to take particular delight in strafing farmers in their fields and travelers on the roads. What we didn't know as we moved east was that Hitler and Stalin had made a secret pact to divide Poland in half at the River Bug, with the eastern part going to the Russians and the western part to the Germans. By September 17 the Russian Red Army began moving westward into Poland. So, much to our surprise, when we reached Bialystok, we found ourselves under Soviet occupation.

I remember how raggedy the Red Army looked when it entered Bialystok. The ordinary Russian soldier "marched" in a disorderly manner, holes in his pants and shirt, a rifle hung over his shoulder by cord or a piece of frayed rope. They looked like a collection of beggars. Only the Soviet officers were uniformed halfway decently. What a contrast to the German army I had seen march into Warsaw and would see march into Lemberg (Lvov) twenty-two months later. The Germans were ferociously equipped and well uniformed—all leather and iron and always marching in step like a drill team. Well, the Russians may have looked ragtag and ill equipped, but they showed later that they could fight effectively with whatever they had.

Whether under Polish, Russian, or German control, life went on. In occupied Bialystok a Russian conductor, Mikhail Zacharovich Shepper, organized an extraordinary symphony orchestra, with which I performed, on one occasion playing Tchaikovsky's Piano Concerto no. 1 in B-flat Minor. However, Bialystok's musicians remembered Shepper for something entirely different than his praiseworthy accomplishment of organizing a symphony orchestra under those difficult conditions. Since none of us had white tie and tails, each member of the orchestra, including Shepper, performed in regular dark business clothes. But this was not good enough for Shepper. He wanted to conduct us in his own grand monkey suit. So he found a poor Jewish tailor in Bialystok and convinced him to make a formal suit with tails. The fellow did it, somehow finding all the necessary fine wool material, a nearly impossible feat. Shepper collected his custom-made tails and soon afterward returned to Moscow without paying the tailor a single zloty.

I had been living in Bialystok for about three or four weeks when a colleague from my class at the Warsaw Conservatory arrived from Lemberg, also occupied by the Russians. He told me that Professor Drzewiecki was now teaching there at the Conservatory. That was all I needed to hear. I packed my bags and took the next train to Lemberg.

Refugee in Lemberg

In Lemberg I immediately became one more of that city's thousands of homeless refugees constantly struggling to find a place to sleep at night. Luckily for me, my sister Lucy and I had attended a student camp the summer before where we had met a couple from Lemberg, Herman Zozowski and his wife, who was also a pianist. When I telephoned them, Herman acted as if he had been expecting my call. His maid had just left, he said, so I could have her bed in the kitchen. That was worth a fortune, I assure you. People were sleeping on benches in the park and anywhere else they could find a place to put their head down. I heard stories about people renting space in big dresser drawers and sleeping with their feet hanging out. And I had a place to stay with a bed!

The next day when I found Professor Drzewiecki, he told me, "*Now* you are going to graduate!" He immediately took me to the Conservatory office, where I filled out the application form. The next morning he asked, "What did you put down as the profession of your father?"

"Businessman."

"No, no," he said. "They'll throw you out of the Conservatory. This is *communism!* Let's go back." So we went back to the Conservatory office, where he retrieved my application, tore it up, and had me fill out a new one. I wrote that my father was a worker. Otherwise, I would not have been accepted.

At first, the Soviet system seemed pretty good to me. Rents were low, and I got to hear for free the great artists Moscow sent to perform at the Conservatory. However, we soon found out what Russian communism was really like. They always had to know everything about you. "Political officers" were stationed everywhere, including at the Conservatory, watching and listening to every little thing you did and said. After a while you became afraid to open your mouth for fear somebody would denounce you, and then off you would go on the next train to Siberia for no reason except that you had expressed an opinion.

In early 1940 Professor Drzewiecki told me he had enough and had decided to return to Warsaw. Not legally, of course. People were being smuggled across the Bug River. He told me he had written a letter to the rector of the Lemberg Conservatory, a Ukrainian by the name of Dr. Vasyl Barvynsky, a very fine composer, saying that his mother was dying and that he was leaving to attend her funeral but would be back. Of course, his mother wasn't dying, but if he was caught at the border between the Russian and German sectors, he would have a somewhat legitimate excuse for trying to go west.

By then I had become his assistant, so he told me to take his class and keep it going so that it looked as if he would return. He would then let me know when he made it to Warsaw, even though the mails were very uncertain. When I took over his class, all the other professors were very upset—"He's only a graduate student! What right has he to teach?" Professor Drzewiecki had the best students, which I inherited, so the other professors wanted to kill me. I taught the class for about two weeks until the news arrived that Professor Drzewiecki was safe in Warsaw and wasn't coming back. So the class was disbanded.

I was in constant danger of being picked up by the Russians and sent to Siberia. The Russians did not accept the concept of Polish refugees. They declared that either we had to stay in their sector and become citizens, or they would send us to the Germans in the western part of Poland. Nobody knew for certain how much validity we should give to this declaration. People survived more by follow-ing rumors than official statements, and Soviet statements could never be trusted, anyway. A now familiar joke about two Soviet newspapers summed up our feeling at the time: there were two main papers, *Pravda* (Truth) and *Isvestia* (News). People said, "If you buy the *Truth*, you can't find the news in it, and if you buy the *News*, you can't find the truth in it."

Everything was very unsettled, and on top of all this I received a letter from my mother—it was a miracle that it got through. She basically said, "Don't go inside the Soviet Union because you'll never get out of there. Keep away from communism." She didn't write it exactly like that because it would never have passed the censors, but she managed to make me understand what she meant. She was the most wonderful mother who ever lived.

The Russians set up places at various Lemberg schools for refu-gees to register to return to western Poland. I hoped to rejoin my parents and teacher, so I voluntarily walked into one and registered to go back to Warsaw. The first question they asked was, "Where do you live?" I answered all their questions and gave them all the information they wanted. The only problem now was that if they wanted to come for me, they would know exactly where to find me. When the time arrived for those of us who had registered to return to Warsaw, the Germans sent only one or two freight trains of refu-gees west, leaving thousands of the rest of us behind. All of a sud-den, we were stranded—stateless people without papers.

After I registered with the Russians, I moved from Herman's apartment into a magnificent apartment owned by Dr. Stefania Lobaczewska, née von Festenburg, who was professor of music history at the Conservatory and one of the great ladies of music in Poland. She was a communist, even though she was from the Austrian elite, the "upper ten thousand." In fact, she was a princess. She lived in a beautiful six-room flat, with two bathrooms and two separate entrances, at Smolki Plaza 4. Wide marble stairways led to her fourth-floor doorway. A luxury automobile showroom occupied the building's first floor. My favorite room was her salon—a huge room that held her beautiful Steinway grand piano. The only problem was that an awful Russian had moved in, uninvited, with his family and was now living there too.

Dr. Lobaczewska's husband, a seventy-two-year-old retired colonel in the Polish army, was "lost." The day after the Russians occupied Lemberg, Soviet soldiers had come to their apartment and told her husband to get ready. They took him away, and she never heard from him again. Perhaps he met the same fate as the thousands of Polish officers whose bodies were later discovered in the mass grave at Katyn. She never found out how the Russians found him so quickly.

I once said to her, "Dr. Lobaczewska, you've lost your husband in such a horrible way, and yet you're a communist. I don't get it." She said, "Communism is a revolutionary idea, and in all revolutions there are always victims." That was her philosophy.

A few days after they took her husband away, the awful Russian knocked on her door. When the maid opened it, he pushed past her. He was a terrible fellow named Ishchuk who worked as a Soviet jailer for the NKVD, the People's Commissariat of Internal Affairs—the predecessor to the KGB. In Poland there was a saying that NKVD meant "Never Know When You Come Back." They took you just the way the Gestapo took you. The thug announced to Dr. Lobaczewska that he was going to be living in her apartment, and she'd better not argue about it. He chose the salon, the biggest, most beautiful room, with four large windows, and moved in with his wife and two young children. And that was that. Who could Dr.

Lobaczewska complain to? The piano was moved into the dining room.

Professor Drzewiecki had been good friends with Dr. Lobaczewska and had been staying with her before he returned to Warsaw. When it became clear that her husband would probably not be coming back, Dr. Lobaczewska, afraid of being alone with this Russian thug, asked me to find another student and share her apartment with her. So a colleague, George Goldflam, and I joined the professor.

The only room available for us was a small guest room with one bed. Its window had been blown out during the bombing of Lemberg. Although George and I covered the broken window with cardboard, we succeeded only in keeping the light out, not stopping the freezing winter cold. And it was an especially horrible and cold winter, with temperatures reaching minus thirty degrees. At night we took turns getting under the covers first to try to warm up the bed. Then the other one would pile every loose piece of clothing we owned on top of the covers and jump in. Getting out of bed in the morning was like jumping into an ice-cold shower.

Then another Russian, an instructor in antiaircraft or something, moved in and took over another room. What a slimy character he was! He was always drunk and always after Dr. Lobaczewska, wanting to force himself on her and rape her. He'd come staggering in with a bottle of vodka in his hand and demand, "Where's the lady? Where's the lady of the house?" I'd say, "She's out," or "Not about," or "Up on the moon," or anything that came to mind. We had two bathrooms in the apartment, one in the front and one in the back near the kitchen. When Dr. Lobaczewska heard him coming, she would lock herself in the bathroom. Then, while he was looking for her, I would try to distract him. "What do you want an old woman for?" I'd say to him. "C'mon, go get yourself a nice twenty-year-old girl."

One night I picked up his bottle of vodka, which was sitting on the table, and just started walking toward his room. He said,

"Gimme the vodka! I want a drink!" I didn't say anything, just kept on walking. When he saw the bottle moving, he fixed his eyes on it and began following it like he was mesmerized. He followed me into his room, where I put the bottle down on his table and said, "There's your vodka. Have a drink!" I walked out and shut the door. That was it for that night. He would keep drinking until he passed out. I was saving Dr. Lobaczewska almost every night.

While I was staying at her place, George Raizler, a lawyer and friend of Dr. Lobaczewska, whose own place had been pretty much bombed out, used to come over to use our bathroom. He would always beg me to play the piano for him while he took a bath. So I would oblige and play his favorite Chopin and Brahms pieces while he soaked in the tub. Years later our paths crossed again when George became the prosecuting attorney for the Nazi crimes committed at Majdanek.

Rumors began spreading that the Russians were preparing to send all refugees without Soviet citizenship or some kind of a Soviet passport to Siberia. My roommate, George Goldflam, was safe enough since he had managed to become a citizen and obtain a passport, even though it had the lousy paragraph 11 in it, which made it illegal to reside in a big city or within two hundred kilometers of the border. Despite paragraph 11, George stayed in Lemberg. He was an orphan from Warsaw who felt himself relatively fortunate in his new situation. Because he knew how to play jazz, he had managed to find work playing piano in a Russian military café during their late afternoon cocktail hour. That meant extra income. George was no communist, but, as he said to me once, "I have no reason to go back. Go back to what? Here, at least I'm surviving. What's to come, will come."

My friend Herman, with whom I had stayed earlier, received a regular passport and Soviet citizenship, whether he wanted it or not, by virtue of the fact that he was a native Lemberger. He had gotten himself a job as an administrator in Lemberg's Ministry of Housing, a city hall job that probably saved my life. One day while

I was at the Conservatory, the little brother of Herman's wife came running up to me all out of breath. "Herman sent me! Herman sent me! Herman says, 'Don't you dare sleep at home tonight.' Come to Herman's for dinner." Herman was a very serious fellow, and I trusted him completely. So that evening I did not return to my apartment and instead went to Herman's.

When I arrived, Herman said to me, "Boy, are you lucky you know me. I was in City Hall today turning in rent money to my boss, and the door to the NKVD room was open. I heard the Russians say, 'We are beginning tonight.'" We both knew what that meant. They were going to start rounding up refugees without passports and send them to Siberia.

"They may come for you tonight," Herman said. "Sleep here, and tomorrow morning we'll find out."

So I spent the night at Herman's. The next morning as I approached the Conservatory, George was there yelling at me, "You son-of-a-gun! Because of you I almost went to Siberia last night!" The Soviet police had come at two in the morning, hammering and pounding on the door with fists and rifle butts. George let them in, and two soldiers with bayonets on their rifles grabbed him. "You're Filar. Get dressed."

"No, no," he said. "My name is Goldflam. Look at my passport." He gave the soldiers his passport, but they wouldn't read it. Maybe they couldn't read it.

"Nyet! You're Filar. Come with us!"

Just then Ishchuk, the Russian living in the salon, came wandering out in his underwear. "Nyet, nyet. This is not Filar. I know what Filar looks like. This is Goldflam. Don't worry, I'll find Filar for you myself." They let George go, thank God, but now I had a personal Russian enemy who had taken it on himself to find me.

And Ishchuk was a horrible guy. He worked in the jails for the NKVD or one of those organizations—they kept changing their name and initials, but whatever the letters, they always meant the same thing. If they took you away, you probably were never going to come back. But why would he go to the trouble to search for me? He had nothing against me. I figured he probably wanted to get rid of all of us so he could grab that gorgeous apartment for himself. At least I had now been warned, so I could now be on the alert.

About ten other Conservatory students had the same problem of statelessness, so we all went into hiding, sleeping at night wherever we could. I usually stayed with Herman. By day we would slip in to attend our classes at the Conservatory. The Conservatory's director, Professor Barvynsky, knew our situation and let us continue taking classes, although we understood that if we were caught, he could not help us.

One morning I was sitting in a streetcar headed to the Conservatory when I saw Ishchuk waiting to board at the next stop. He stepped up onto the streetcar, and because he was in his uniform, he was allowed to stand on the front platform. Thank God, he didn't turn around and see me. I started to push back through a crowd of people toward the rear platform, intending to jump off. Just then the woman conductor began yelling at me, "Why are you trying to go back there? It's not allowed! You know you have to get off in front."

I whispered, "Look at who is in front. I *have* to jump off in the back."

She looked at Ishchuk in his uniform and understood. Suddenly, she became very busy demanding everybody's ticket in a loud voice—"Tickets! Tickets! Let me see your tickets now!" and waved her arms around to create a diversion to keep Ishchuk from seeing me.

I jumped off the back of the streetcar and ran toward the Conservatory, hiding in the entrance of the building opposite so I could observe the street. Sure enough, a minute later, Ishchuk turned the corner. He had obviously come there looking for me. He wasn't inside the Conservatory very long before I saw him being hustled out by another Russian, the Soviet political representative at the Conservatory. "Go to hell!" the political rep shouted. "Come here again threatening the director, and I'll send *you* to Siberia!" I smiled. That was about as sweet as it gets.

There was a recital hall at the Lemberg Conservatory, not as large or as beautiful as Warsaw's, certainly, but still a recital hall. All the great Russian artists played there. I heard performances by David Oistrakh; Emil Gilels; Rosa Tamarkina; Jakov Zak, who won first prize in Poland's Chopin Competition; and many marvelous Russian female opera singers. The music was wonderful! One night I attended a concert dressed in my best dark suit. As I was leaving, around 10:30, to take the forty-five minute streetcar ride to Herman's, the streetlights suddenly went out, and air raid sirens began wailing. This meant that within fifteen minutes everyone had to be at home. The police would be stopping people on the street—"Give me your documents! Are you a citizen or not?" If you weren't a citizen, forget it. You were on your way to Siberia.

What was I going to do? I didn't have a prayer of getting home without being stopped, so I decided that my best chance was to hide at the Conservatory. I backtracked along an outside passageway to the rear of the building and found steps that led down into a part of the basement. In the darkness I discovered a second set of steps leading up to a door, barred from the inside, which was located at the back of the recital hall's stage. Since this door had a few holes in it, I could look directly into the hall's foyer. It was pitch-black, and there was all sorts of disgusting trash, attracting a swarm of rats. In spite of the filth and rats, I decided to stay put, figuring that this was as good a place as any to hide. If I saw anyone come into the hall, I could dash down the steps and make a run for it along the side passageway. It wasn't much of a plan, but it was the best I had. So I settled in on the top step to wait until daylight or until it was safe enough for me to make my way to Herman's.

I had been sitting there in the darkness for quite some time, just listening, when at about two in the morning I heard a sudden pounding sound on the hall's main doors. From his little apartment in the Conservatory, the old superintendent emerged in his fur coat to see who was banging on the door. "Who is it?"

"NKVD. Open up." I started to shake, thinking they were coming for me. Why else would the secret police be there? Someone must have seen me go into the basement. I listened as they shouted their orders: "Open the recital hall, leave the lights on. We'll be back." Then they left, and I saw through the holes the old man hobbling back in my direction. He set up a table and four or five chairs no more than two yards from where I was hiding.

Soon the Russians returned. I heard trucks coming to a halt at the front entrance and the sounds of people being unloaded. They herded those who had been caught in that night's roundup into the recital hall to be processed for Siberia. I could see everything. Each person went up to the table, where Russian NKVD officials demanded that he or she produce some document that he or she didn't have. Many were crying, pleading. They knew where they were being sent. "I'm not against your government," they would say, or "I'm not against anybody. I have a sick wife in Warsaw," or "I have an old mother in Cracow. I just want to go home to my family." Always the response was "Shut up!" All their entreaties were ignored.

I watched in horrified silence as the NKVD processed more than two hundred people. If I had moved or made a single sound, the Russians at the table would have heard me, and that would have been it for me. I sat there frozen, silent as a dead man.

About five in the morning the trucks came back for the people who had been processed. They were loaded back on the trucks and taken to a train headed to Siberia. The Russians left, and the hall was locked up and returned to normal, as if nothing had happened. I was the only witness to the whole thing. And there was never a word in the papers about any of this, of course. The people just disappeared into thin air.

I finally emerged from my hiding place about seven o'clock, stiff and cramped. My suit was filthy, and I looked terrible, like some sort of vagrant. I brushed off my clothes and smoothed my hair and cleaned my face with saliva as best I could, so they wouldn't stop me on the street. Trying to look as inconspicuous as possible, I took a streetcar back to Herman's. He was eating breakfast with his wife when I came in.

"Where were you?" he asked in amazement. "Do you know how lucky you are? The Russians came into our neighborhood last night. Marian, they went from house to house, from room to room. If you had been sleeping here, you'd be on your way to Siberia right now."

Musical Worker

Through it all I managed to keep attending classes at the Conservatory without getting captured. Then one day the director called the ten students without passports into his office. He had very good news. He told us he had managed to acquire documents from the military governor stating that we were "musical workers" needed by the state. Now we had papers. Now we were safe. Now nobody could touch us.

That night I finally went back home to Dr. Lobaczewska's apartment. When I turned my key and opened the door, who should be standing there but Ishchuk, my Russian tormentor. But I wasn't afraid of him anymore. He was dumbfounded to see me come back. "Where were you?" he asked.

This was my moment, and I couldn't resist. "Oh, I met this wonderful, wonderful girl, and, well, you know how it is. God, she is so beautiful! You'd be jealous if you saw her." He tried to take that in, but I don't think he got it. All he could say was, "You don't live here anymore."

"Oh? You think so?" I walked past him and went to my room.

After I saw firsthand how the Russians rounded up refugees and sent them to Siberia, I thought I should try to warn my brother Michael and my sister Lucy and her husband Ben in Bialystok. I went to the basement of the main Lemberg post office and filled out a telegram form, handing it to a beautiful young lady about my age. Of course, I couldn't write, "The Russians are sending people to Siberia," so I wrote, "Watch out! You can get terribly sick," which apparently wasn't very clever. The young lady at the window took one look at my telegram and said to me in a low voice, "I'll pay for it. Now run, before they read it and catch you."

"Thank you," I said. "I'll be back." I got out of there as fast as I could. After I received my "musical worker" document, I went back to the post office and paid for the telegram. I thanked the girl for her help and took her to lunch. We became good friends. Later, after the Germans entered Lemberg, she came to my apartment and, fully aware of the risks she would be taking, offered to hide me. I was very grateful to her, this lovely Polish girl, but I had to refuse her offer. My parents in Warsaw needed me more than ever. I couldn't abandon them.

Unfortunately, my telegram wasn't enough to save Michael, Lucy, or Ben from capture, for they too had registered to return to Warsaw, and when the Germans didn't take them back, the Russians came after them. First they grabbed Michael and sent him to Siberia. Then, a few nights later, they came and took Lucy and Ben away. They sent Michael to one gulag and Lucy and her husband to another. As bad as Siberia was, however, it saved them from later getting captured by the Germans.

In Siberia they forced Lucy to walk ten miles each day to her workstation, where they made her saw wood in subzero weather. One day her husband, trudging along next to her, collapsed. "I can't go on," he said. "I can't walk anymore." Lucy, who had been a nurse, rubbed his legs with snow and got him going again before the guards came and shot him. Later, when she became too weak and ill to work, the authorities said that she was faking it and put her in solitary on bread and water. Although she survived Siberia, she never fully recovered her health.

After Professor Drzewiecki returned to Warsaw, I chose as my new Conservatory teacher Professor Halina Levitzka, a Ukrainian. Professor Drzewiecki had recommended that I work with her, saying that she wouldn't be able to teach me all that much, but whatever she said wouldn't be detrimental either. Professor Levitzka was happy to have me as her pupil and soon found students for me to teach privately. One day she came up to me very excited and happy. "I've found you a Russian big shot," she said, "a general. He has a young son and daughter who want to learn piano. Maybe he can help get your sister and brother out of Siberia." Since I already spoke Russian, I got the job teaching piano to General Antipenko's son Zenia and his daughter Lareczka. I never did learn General Antipenko's first name—no one did. He was very important, and you just didn't ask questions.

In the meantime, I traveled to Bialystok to speak to my brother and sister's landlord. He promised he would send me their addresses in Siberia if he ever heard from them, and, sure enough, in a few weeks I had their addresses. They had written him to find out where in Siberia I had been sent!

I began sending them packages—food, socks, underwear, warm shirts—whatever I could afford. I also sent packages to my parents in Warsaw. All in all, I was doing all right financially, so I was able to help my family. I had a scholarship check every month and private students, I played occasionally on the state radio, and now I taught piano to General Antipenko's children. And by stretching the truth a bit and telling the general that I was a piano tuner (I knew how to pull up a string), I earned extra money tuning the pianos of his friends. Before war broke out between Hitler and Stalin, I was thus able to earn enough money to keep myself alive and to help my family.

General Antipenko helped me in several other ways, including helping me get rid of that SOB Ishchuk. I wasn't afraid of Ishchuk anymore since I was now legitimate and had important friends, so I thought I ought to pay him back for trying to send me to Siberia. One day I asked General Antipenko for a favor. I could see the antenna come out of his head as I broached the subject. "Now Filar is going to ask for a favor, is he?" "Just a tiny little thing," I said. "We have a Russian living with us, a jailer, and when I practice for my exams, his two little kids come in and pound on the treble with their fingers, and I can't say anything to him. I don't want his room or anything, but couldn't he move in with some of the men he works with, and we get maybe an artist?"

"No problem," he said, and walked to a phone in another room. In a half minute he was back. "A Major Kozlov will handle it. He's in charge of housing. Meet him at City Hall tomorrow morning at eight." Kozlov was the quartermaster for the military in the city and a beautiful guy. He looked ten feet tall. The next day we walked together from City Hall to my building and entered through the courtyard so everyone would see us together.

When the major went in to talk with Ishchuk, I explained to Dr. Lobaczewska that we were getting rid of Ishchuk. "You're crazy," she said. "You can't kick out a Russian."

"You'll see," I said.

Ishchuk left with his wife and two kids and didn't make a fuss. He was just a sergeant or something. Later, when the Germans occupied the city, I happened to see him again, and again he was waiting at a streetcar stop. But this time he was in civilian clothes.

One week after the Germans began their attack against the Soviet Union on June 22, 1941, I graduated summa cum laude from the State Conservatory. As the Germans were bombing Lemberg, the candidates for graduation went to the basement of the Conservatory to perform their final exams. Two concert grand Steinways were placed in the basement, and I played a recital of Bach, Beethoven's Sonata Op. 109, Schumann's *Carnaval*, Chopin's B Minor Sonata, and the Tchaikovsky B-flat Minor Piano Concerto, as well as some Debussy.

The outbreak of war between the Germans and Russians made me flat broke. In fact, since I was fully expecting to receive more than three thousand rubles on the first of the month, I had just borrowed fifty rubles from my friend George so I could send another package to my family. But as the Germans approached and bombed Lemberg, the Russians retreated with their rubles, and suddenly I was without funds.

Before the retreat began, I went to General Antipenko to ask if it was true that the Red Army was leaving. "Yes, it's true," he said, "but we'll be back. We'll get the Germans inside Russia, just like we did Napoleon. We'll beat the living hell out of them and then take Berlin." Which is exactly what they did.

"I'll be glad to take you to Moscow," he said. "You have a half hour. Go home and pack a small suitcase, just a little one. You'll sit next to the driver." So I went home to pack, but on the way I thought about my wonderful parents and how they needed me. So I decided against going to Moscow. I wonder sometimes what would have been my story if I had gone.

Now that the Russians were leaving, how were we going to survive? And without any money? The Conservatory was closed, and I was without students. When George told me he had been fired from his job at the café because of the war, I exploded. "Use your head! Do you want to starve? We've got nothing! Go back to the café and tell them you're a food specialist, a restaurant manager, a chef, anything!"

So he went back, and, thank God, he came home with the keys to a food storeroom of which, as luck had it, they had put him in charge. A few days later, as the Germans were entering the city, we went to the storeroom at six in the morning and began to clean it out—and I don't mean we were sweeping the floor. We packed up all the food we could carry, plus every sort of vodka and spirit, all the wine, and, of course, all the cigarettes, which were sort of a wartime currency, especially with Polish peasants. As we were carrying things out of the storeroom, the superintendent of the building came running up to us. "Hey, you damn Jews! What do you think you are doing here? I'm going to call the Germans!"

"Not so fast, Mister," I said to him. "If the Germans come, they'll take everything, won't they? You'll have nothing, and we'll have nothing. How about we split fifty-fifty?"

"You've got a deal," the old guy said. So together the three of us cleaned out the storeroom of everything eatable, drinkable, or smokable—everything except a big container of stinking hard-boiled eggs. Everything else became ours. We took our share back to our room and stocked the place from floor to the ceiling with cans and bottles. If a shell had ever hit, we would have drowned!

The janitor of our building had a brother who was a farmer, so when the Germans arrived, this farmer started coming into the city with his horse and cart looking for cigarettes, spirits, or wine to buy and sell. We did business with him and got something to eat in return. Keeping the farmer happy also kept us on the right side of our janitor. I was in the janitor's good graces anyway because I was tutoring his son in music theory. His school grades were pretty bad until he started working with me. When he brought home an A (he had never received higher than a C), his father was delighted.

When the Germans marched into Lemberg, they had Ukrainian SS volunteers with them. The day after the Germans occupied Lemberg, they turned the Ukrainians loose, and in the pogrom that followed they killed Jews left and right. In the meantime, the Germans created an economy in which non-Jews received salaries while Jews didn't get anything. If George and I hadn't cleaned out the storeroom, we would have starved to death.

The Germans' first order to the population was "Everybody back to work!" Since they had closed the Conservatory, that put me in a tight spot. A Jewish gentleman who lived in our building, Mr. Rappaport, a very nice man with a wife and a child, suggested that I work with him in his office located just across from our building on Kollontaja Street. He said he'd find me something to do so that I'd have an actual job, which might help legitimize my status in the eyes of the Germans.

The state store he managed was on the main floor, next to the courtyard gate. When I first entered it, I immediately thought, "This is a bad location. If the Germans come, they can jump us without warning, and there would be no chance to run." Before I even finished my thought, two Ukrainians in SS uniforms walked in, and other Ukrainians bicycled into the courtyard.

One of the SS demanded Mr. Rappaport's papers, but he refused. He questioned their right to ask him for anything and gave them a bad time in Ukrainian. It wasn't the wisest thing to do, but it was lucky for me. The bandit who was confronting me went over to help out with Mr. Rappaport. While the Ukrainians were concentrating on him, I made a break for it. I ran up the stairs to the balcony and headed for the top floor, as SS men arrived and went up to all the floors. When I reached the top floor, there was an SS man on the top floor but on the opposite side of the courtyard, quite a distance away. He pointed at me and shouted, "Catch him! Catch him!" I pointed back at him and yelled, "Catch him! Catch him!" Anything to cause confusion, and there was a lot of it.

With the SS in the courtyard shouting at me to halt, I ran along the balcony until I saw an open door and burst in. A maid was sitting in the kitchen washing her legs in a basin, her skirt all the way up to her hips. "Hey, don't yell," I said to her, hoping to calm her obvious fright. "I'm not going to hurt you. I just need to hide." I didn't wait for an answer. A bedroom door was open, so I ran in and scrambled under the bed.

The Ukrainian SS worked their way up through the building, searching all the floors and questioning a lot of people who had come to the upper floors thinking that they would be safe. The SS actually went into the apartment where I was hiding. I heard them tramping around and held my breath. Fortunately, they didn't bother looking under the bed—another lucky break for me.

Mr. Rappaport wasn't so fortunate. They took him to jail, where they grabbed his wallet, stole his money, took his watch, and almost killed him. One of the Ukrainians saw Mr. Rappaport's gold wedding ring and demanded it. Mr. Rappaport tried to take it off, but his finger had thickened through the years, and he couldn't remove the ring. The Ukrainian SS bandit handed him a knife. "Cut your finger off," he said. Mr. Rappaport pleaded for his finger and tried harder to pull the ring off. He kept working at it, using his saliva, until the ring finally came off. He then handed over his wedding ring of twenty years. When he came back home, he was a broken man.

In December 1941 I received a letter from my parents saying they were sending a "guide" to bring me back to Warsaw. By this time a Jew needed the guidance of an expert in deception to travel by train. The day before I was to leave I walked to the train station to get a schedule, but as I approached the station, I saw German soldiers. So I turned and started to walk back, when all of a sudden a Jewish fellow, standing next to the gate of a big courtyard, called out to me, "Come here. You'll go to work."

"Go to hell," I said. Then an armed SS man stepped out from behind the gate. "Hey, you! Come here!" What a trick, sending a Jew to catch a Jew! But it had worked, and I quickly found myself in a courtyard with more than a hundred other people, each of us being readied for the camp on Janowska Street, a horrible place already infamous in Lemberg for killing people.

They formed us into a column five people wide and marched us down the street with the German SS man leading the column and the Jew who had turned me in keeping an eye on the rear. When I saw that we were headed in the direction of where I lived with Dr. Lobaczewska on Smolki Platz, I said to myself, "They aren't going to take me. I'm going to escape."

The first thing I knew I had to do was change my position in the formation. I had started out in the middle of the marching columns, but as silently and as inconspicuously as possible I changed places with each guy behind me until I had moved from the middle of the column to the back. I wanted to be able to slip away if and when my chance came. As we approached Kollontaja Street, I crossed my fingers and prayed for luck. I had an escape plan in my mind that I wanted to try, and I hoped God was with me. Kollontaja Street intersected with Smolki Platz, and I lived at Smolki Platz 4. If the column made a right turn, we'd be heading directly down Kollontaja for Smolki Platz, and I could then make a break for it. Luck was with me. We turned right.

Now things got even more interesting. There were entrances to the courtyard of Smolki Platz 4 at Kollontaja 2 and Kollontaja 4, so I now had two choices. I could run through either of the entrances on Kollontaja Street and then dash across the large open courtyard to where I lived, but I would be an easy target for anyone with a gun. Or I could gamble and hope that we would make a left turn onto Smolki Platz, where I could then run straight up to my front door. I decided not to run for it at Kollontaja 2 or 4 but instead to gamble that we would turn left. I prayed for luck and got it again. We turned left and headed straight for where I lived!

As we passed the main gate in front of my apartment house, I casually stepped out of the column. On each side of the entrance gate were two ornamental pieces of sculpture. I put my foot up on one as if to fix my shoelace, but actually to check if the SS man was watching and to weigh my chances. The Jew guarding the rear saw me, but he kept his mouth shut. All this time the German SS man leading the column hadn't looked around once, but now suddenly he heard or sensed something. I looked right just as he looked left— and he saw me. It was now or never. I was off like a shot. "Halt!" he called and pulled out his pistol. "Kiss my you know what!" I yelled in Polish. I remember wondering for a split second how the damn German felt to have a Jew escaping from him, but I didn't have much time to think about it. I flew up those beautiful white marble stairs as if I had wings on my heels and was on the fourth floor in a minute with my key in hand. "Dr. Lobaczewska," I said as I burst in, "the Germans are after me."

"Don't worry, they won't get you," she said. "Get inside."

The Germans knocked on every door in our building and stayed quite a while, searching for me. When they came to our door, Dr. Lobaczewska said, "Nichts Juden! Nichts Juden! [No Jews here! No Jews here!]" Eventually, the column marched on without me.

The next day my guide arrived. I took off my Star of David and shaved my hair on the sides of my head so that when I wore a hat no one could tell if I had blond hair or black hair. About nine that evening we boarded the night train to Warsaw, a local train scheduled to arrive around six the next morning. Strangely, while my guide definitely looked like a Jew to me, nobody seemed to take notice of him. I suppose that was because he just looked like an ordinary Joe, a simple guy who might sell newspapers on the street. But while I looked a lot less Jewish than he did, an off-duty Polish railroad man sitting opposite us in our compartment took a big interest in me. He looked at me and kept looking at me, and the way he was looking at me made me think to myself, "Uh-oh. He smells a Jew. I'm in trouble."

I went out into the corridor to get away from him, but a minute later, as I was lighting a cigarette, he came out and stood right next to me, his face next to mine, his eyes staring into my eyes. He kept his mouth shut, but I was sure he was thinking, "I've got you, Jew." It occurred to me that the only thing that might save me now was my big mouth because I was sure I spoke better Polish than he did and had a better Polish accent than he could ever dream of having. Also, I knew all the tough slang that was used in the poorer neighborhoods by less educated people.

So I started to talk. I pulled out my pack of cigarettes and said, "Pan szanowny paloncy? [Do you smoke?]" At the sound of my accent, he sort of stepped back and stared at me. Jews didn't sound like that. I gave him a cigarette, lit it, and began talking as fast as I could. I talked about Warsaw, about the weather, and about the passing scene, and then I started telling him Polish jokes—not Polack jokes, Polish jokes. The wrinkles on his forehead gradually started to straighten, and all of a sudden we were pals and he was telling me about how he cheats on his wife—real buddy-buddy. We talked through the night, and at one point he told me how he brought Jews to the Gestapo and how the Gestapo shot them in front of him. And how he got vodka or ham for it. He said to me, "You know, I just go like this—sniff—and I smell a Jew a mile away."

"A mile away?" I said. "I can smell 'em *two* miles away." I made myself out a worse anti-Semite than he was.

Meanwhile, our local train was stopping at every town, and there were German military police on each train platform. All he would have had to do was call one and say, "I've got a Jew here," and I would have been dead.

We made it to Warsaw at 6:30 in the morning, and while he was saying good-bye to me, he made his little confession that at first he had thought I was Jewish. "Hey, hey, Mister," I said, "slow down there. Don't be insulting your friends. I might not like it." And then we shook hands. "I hope I see you again sometime," I said. Sure I did. I hoped he'd be struck by lightning.

The Warsaw Ghetto

When I arrived back in Warsaw after being away for more than two years, it was bitterly cold, and things were very different. When I left, there had not been a ghetto. There was a Jewish neighborhood, but Jews lived in every part of the city. Before the war Warsaw had more than one million people, a third of them Jews. While I had been in Lemberg, the Germans had collected Jews from Warsaw, its suburbs, and all the nearby towns and put them together in what was to be the ghetto. Then they built a ten-foot-high wall around it. They wanted us all in one place so they could murder us more easily. But we didn't know that yet.

My guide took me to a very large hole in the ghetto wall where a Polish policeman stood guard. Because the Germans had ordered that Jews give up their fur coats for the German army freezing in Russia, Poles went into the ghetto to buy fur coats cheaply. They didn't know that in a few weeks they would have to turn over their own fur coats. So the guide and I walked up to the policeman and said we wanted to go in to buy fur coats. I gave him some money and said that when we came out there would be more. As we stepped through the wall, a Jewish policeman came up to me. "Hey, you came through the hole. Give me *szmalcowe* [some money]."

"I'm Jewish," I said. "Beat it!"

It must have been about seven in the morning when I arrived "home" at 72 Sienna Street. Since incendiary bombs had destroyed the building on Gesia Street we lived in before the war, my family was now living in the apartment of my uncle Joe Frankle, who had left for Bialystok with his wife and two children to join his wife's family. Bombs had torn off the front of the building, but the rest of it was still standing. I went upstairs and knocked on the kitchen door. I heard my dad say, "Who is it?"

"It's me, Dad! Open up!" He tried to open the door but couldn't. They had placed an iron bar across it, and the weather was so cold that the bar had frozen against the door. I heard him call to my mother, "Where's the hammer? Where's the hammer?"

"In the bathroom," I heard her say. Just hearing my mother's voice made me cry.

When my dad opened the door, I fell into his arms. It was still very early—and extremely cold—and everyone was still in bed except my father. I took off my outer clothes and jumped into my mother's bed and kissed her hand for about half an hour without stopping. Then I cried some more and turned around and fell sound asleep.

We had a wonderful reunion, but something was wrong. My sister Helen had hugged me joyously when I went to her bed, but she stayed there. When we ate breakfast, Helen didn't join us. At noon she was still in bed. "Helen," I said, "what's wrong? Are you sick? Do you have a cold or something?"

"Oh, I'll get up a little later." My parents looked away and didn't say anything.

Helen was very, very beautiful, with lovely blond hair. After the Germans marched into Warsaw, they began looking for Polish army officers, who were now civilians since there no longer was a functioning Polish army. The officers with Jewish friends got smart and went into the ghetto with their wives to hide. They put a Star of David on their coats and pretended they were Jews. The Germans got wind of it and began stopping people in the ghetto who didn't look Jewish. My sister didn't look Jewish. Three months before my return, the Gestapo grabbed her on the street. "Where's your husband?" they demanded of her. "He's a Polish officer, isn't he?"

"I'm Jewish," she had said. "I'm single."

They slapped her. "You're lying."

They took her to Gestapo headquarters on Szucha Avenue and threatened her, saying they were going to beat the hell out of her and kill her. Few people walked out alive. As a result of the horror she went through there, her spine was damaged, and she became semiparalyzed from the waist down. Whenever she got out of bed, she couldn't stand up straight. Holding onto the tops of chairs, she would go one hand over the other around the kitchen table.

What kind of Warsaw had I come back to? You can't imagine. You go away for a short time, and when you return, the building you lived in is no longer standing, your sister is half paralyzed, and the Germans have confiscated your father's business.

Banks did not exist anymore. When the Nazis closed the banks and stole everyone's savings, the only money people had was what was left in their pockets. When they spent whatever was in their pocket, they were finished. That was it.

And now there was a ghetto, and it was hell. That winter was particularly cold and difficult, and food was scarce. Among the many creative things my father did to feed his family was somehow, somewhere find a few live fish, which he kept in our bathtub. I can't describe how odd it felt the first time I entered our bathroom and saw fish swimming and flopping around in the tub. But it wasn't funny. It meant we had lost everything. We were lucky to have the fish. And I didn't particularly like fish.

A short time after my return, I learned there was a Jewish Symphony Orchestra in the ghetto, a wonderful orchestra made up of former members of the Warsaw Philharmonic and conducted by Marian Neutajch, a cellist who had been the concertmaster of the State Radio Symphony. The orchestra played to full houses in a beautiful new cinema, the Kino Femina, on the corner of Leszno and Solna Streets. The Femina had been built just before the war began, but it had never opened because of a law declaring that any place of amusement had to be a certain number of feet away from a church, and there was a Catholic church on the corner that was one foot too close. But now that there were no Catholics in the ghetto, the Femina could be used for performances of the Jewish Symphony Orchestra. I met with Neutajch, and he asked me to play.

I particularly remember one performance, for several reasons. For one thing, my family attended—my mother and father, my brother Joel with his wife Ala, my sister Helen, and my brother Ignaz with his wife Mina and their three-year-old, Kubus, a beautiful little boy. This was the last time they were all together to hear me perform.

Neutajch planned to have me play the Tchaikovsky concerto, but since Jews were only allowed to play Jewish composers, he announced on the sign that the symphony would perform the Mendelssohn concerto. A few days before the scheduled performance, the musicians smuggled their Tchaikovsky scores into Femina Hall. All my music had been lost when our apartment burned, but I was able to play it from memory. So, there within the heart of Nazi-occupied Warsaw, we played "illegally" the music of the great Russian composer Peter Ilyich Tchaikovsky. Most of the scores had been supplied to us by Polish musicians living outside the ghetto and smuggled in through a hole in the ghetto wall. It was risky—the Germans had spies everywhere—but all sorts of things were smuggled through the wall. There was always a hole somewhere and always some kind of contact with the Poles.

These concerts with the symphony were wonderful, but they fed no one. The rations we got from the Germans were a joke. One day Neutajch asked me to join a café trio he was organizing. "I know a professional café violinist who will be our manager. We'll play twice a week for a couple of hours, and he'll get us enough money to buy bread." I said okay and went along with the plan, but since people knew me as a classical pianist, I told him, "I don't want anybody to recognize my face. When I play, I'm going to face the wall." And that's how I played, my back to the audience. After the first performance, I was paid a few zlotys, bought a loaf of bread, and took it home. When my parents asked me how I got the bread, I shrugged it off without explaining.

I also played some violin-piano sonatas in a hall on Lesznost Street with sixteen-year-old violinist David Zaidel, a great talent. We were joined by a fantastically gifted young singer, Marysia Eisenstad, whose father was conductor of the main choir of the Tlomackie Great Synagogue, Warsaw's principal synagogue. My father was a member of that synagogue, and I had sung there in the choir as a kid. When its rabbi, Moses Shorr, made a speech, the mayor of Warsaw would attend. Police on horseback were needed to control the crowds wanting to hear the rabbi. He was an elected member of Poland's senate and a professor of Oriental languages at Warsaw University. His twin sons, Otto and Ludwig, were my classmates. The synagogue was a beautiful building, but the Germans blew it up—it doesn't exist anymore.

In the ghetto I became friends with an old lady who had a piano in her apartment, and I would go there and play for her. I don't remember much about my visits except that it was always dark and she always wore the same clothes. The last time I visited, shortly before the uprising, she handed me some music. "Mr. Filar," she said, "I'm giving you something close to my heart." She had tears in her eyes. "Play it for the rest of your life. It is the most beautiful music in the world." It was Brahms.

Knowing and playing the music of Brahms and other German composers is why many of us in Warsaw had such a hard time believing that the Germans could be murderers. How could they be? They had created such gorgeous music. It didn't make sense. Where did these Nazis come from? Is it possible to play and listen to such music and then murder people?

An estimated one hundred thousand people in the ghetto died of starvation or disease, principally typhus. Dead bodies lay on the sidewalks. Workers with two-wheeled pushcarts collected corpses and took them up to the cemetery for burial in mass graves, legs and arms and hands hanging through the slats of the carts.

I remember one night when I had been visiting somewhere and was returning home about nine o'clock. It was winter and pitch-black because the street lamps didn't work anymore, and there were few lights anywhere. When I reached a corner, I had to look around for a landmark or look up at the sky to see where I was. This evening I was making my way along the street in total darkness, when all of a sudden I felt my right foot step on something soft. I looked down and saw I was standing on a dead man's stomach! I shivered all the way home.

On July 22, 1942, the Germans announced that they were going to "resettle" the Jewish population of Warsaw in the east, where they would get to work and live a normal life. They then told us that anyone who would come to the trains of his own free will would get one pound of bread and two pounds of marmalade. They lied to us beautifully, distracting us with their incredibly formulated deception. Many Jews went because by this time people were dropping dead of starvation in the streets.

About the same time the Germans started forcing some Jews to work for them on the Polish side of the wall. They assigned my brother Joel and me to a group of about 120 Jews working at the railroad station, Warsaw West. It was horrible work, carrying steel rails that weighed a ton, but its importance to the Germans made us valuable and kept us temporarily safe from their stepped-up deportations to Treblinka.

At first, two German railroad men, Mr. Lapsh and Mr. Muller, came into the ghetto to pick us all up at a designated location and march us to work, but around mid-September the Germans forced all the Jewish railroad workers and their families to move into Mila 7, an apartment house in the central ghetto that the Germans had already emptied. Mila 7 was diagonally across the street from Mila 18, which Leon Uris described in his famous novel. Believe me, there were tough, strong cookies in Mila 18, and they were among the ghetto's best smugglers and fighters.

During our first days working at Warsaw West the German guards beat the hell out of us—and I mean beat, opening skulls, not just hitting, rifle butts to the head for no reason. We didn't know what the hell was going on or what they wanted. They didn't say anything, just kept beating us viciously. Finally, we figured it out, and the little group in our department, maybe twenty or thirty of us, collected the few pennies we had among us and gave them money. Then the beatings stopped.

About the second or third day of this, before we understood what the guards wanted, a Polish railroad man came walking over to an SS guard near me and said to him, "I need a Jew for work. *That* one." He pointed at me.

"Go ahead. Take him," the guard said.

I didn't know this guy from Adam, and I couldn't figure out what was going on. When we had walked a safe distance away, he said to me, "Don't worry about a thing. You're a colleague of my son. He studied voice at the Conservatory when you were there." This man was a railroad switchman, and he lived with his wife and son in a house right in the railroad yard. However, I still wasn't sure what it was all about as I followed him into his house.

There was his son, Stan, waiting for me. He thrust his hand out to shake mine. "Hello Marian! How are you? I saw them beating you so I sent my dad out to rescue you." I sat down, and they offered me something to drink and eat. We sang together and had dinner. In fact, we had a ball. I even played the piano. When seven o'clock came around, his father took me back. "This Jew works very well," he told the guard. "I need him tomorrow, too."

"Okay, come get him tomorrow." The guard was totally indifferent. Unfortunately, this situation only lasted couple more days.

We found ways to make this forced labor work for us and help keep us alive. We bribed the two Germans who marched us to work to look the other way while we sold things outside the ghetto. The extra money we managed to take in kept ourselves and our families fed. We would march from Mila 7 through a gate of the ghetto, one guard in front and one in back. As we emerged on the Aryan side, as the Germans called it, young Polish guys with whom we became friends would be waiting for us on the sidewalk. "What do you have today?" they'd ask. "We want shirts. Do you have shirts? Do you have bedsheets? How about towels? Do you have towels?"

Sometimes I'd march out to work with three or four shirts on or a couple of bedsheets wrapped around my belly. Then I'd pull off a shirt and throw it over to someone on the sidewalk. When he caught it, he'd ask what I wanted on the way back. "Bring me a loaf of bread and some potatoes"—I would say that because we were allowed to bring bread and potatoes into the ghetto. Or I might say, "Bring me a pound of butter," or "Bring me some meat." But those things had to be smuggled in.

It wasn't easy to smuggle meat, but we did it. We asked the Poles to cut the meat flat and make a package of it, so we could stuff it along the small of our back between the skin and the belt. If the SS man at the ghetto gate wanted to put his hands back there to search you, you warned him you had lice, and he wouldn't touch you. One time I wore baggy pants and smuggled a whole chicken in for my mother by hanging it between my legs.

Once, when I wanted my mother to have something special, I traded some shirts for a pound of butter. It was a very cold winter day, and I was wearing a raincoat on top of a winter coat. The raincoat pocket had a hole in it, and I dropped the package of butter through the hole and let it fall down to the bottom of the lining. The SS never checked there. I had smuggled food back that way quite a few times. But this time the guard at the ghetto gate caught on, so he checked all the way down the raincoat and found it. "What? You want to eat butter?" he said and slapped me so hard across the face I had finger marks on my cheek for a week. He could have shot me right then and there if he wanted to. Instead, he yelled at me to put the butter in the guardhouse, which was behind him, and get the hell out of there.

When I walked into the guardhouse, I was alone. No one was around. A table was covered with other confiscated packages, so I put my package down, picked up a bigger one, and walked back out into the ghetto. When I got home, I had *two* pounds of butter! "My God," my mother said, laughing, "what did you do? You risked your life."

"To hell with it," I said. "They aren't that smart."

These were days of terror in the ghetto. From July 22 to September 12, 1942, the Germans, often with the collaboration of Jewish police, uprooted the great majority of Jews from Warsaw and deported them in cattle cars to the gas chambers of Treblinka. Only about thirty-five thousand Jews remained in the ghetto by the end of what the Germans called their *Aktion*, with another few thousand "wildcats" in hiding.

I lost my father on August 17, 1942. When I came home from work that day, my mother said, "Father is gone." I said, "What do you mean 'gone'?" He was on his way to a committee meeting when the Germans made a raid inside the ghetto. The SS came in with trucks and blocked off the street my father happened to be walking on, so they got him. Just like that. They put him on a truck along with the other people they trapped that day and took him away. We never heard from him again. Gone. Period.

What is hard to believe is that Jewish police helped take my father away, Jewish police who helped the SS and collaborated with them. Those of us in the ghetto had ways of finding out who were involved. When they took our father, my brother Joel wanted to find the collaborator and kill him.

One night when I was coming home from work at the railway

yards after there had been a raid that morning, I was going down the street where the family of a friend from my gymnasium lived. So I went up to his flat, but no one was there. The place was empty. The doors and windows were open, but it was a dead house. Apparently they had all been deported. Suddenly I saw the little dog who had belonged to the family, and I remembered that her name was Dolly. She seemed glad to see me and was grabbing me by the leg and tugging me here and there. She seemed to want me to go with her, so I went all over the apartment with her, but there was no one there. I decided that I would take her home with me—I've always loved dogs—but when we got to the doorway, she began growling at me even though she had been so friendly before. She refused to leave the house, so that's where she died.

I myself narrowly escaped these raids a couple of times, and once they actually picked me up. I was walking home on a night that was as black as the ace of spades when a Jewish police captain came up and shined an extremely bright light in my eyes.

"What do you think you're doing?" I said. "Stop shining that light in my eyes. I can't see."

He said, "You're under arrest."

"What for?"

The guy just repeated, "You're under arrest." He took me away to a holding station that was next door to where my father's business used to be.

Later that night another policeman who knew me came in. "Marian, what the hell are you doing here?" he asked. "Wait here," he told me. (Where was I going?) "I have to make some arrangements. I can't just let you out." He came back after a while and said, "Beat it." Believe me, I didn't have to be told twice. I would have been off to Treblinka in the morning if this fellow hadn't come along.

After the deportations, the ghetto streets were nearly empty during the day, either because people feared being grabbed by the SS or because all the able-bodied people still in the ghetto worked inside or outside the wall. The people still alive in the ghetto had to be quiet most of the time because the Germans walked around in rubber-soled shoes that made it hard to hear them coming. We put all kinds of junk in front of our apartment house so they would make noise when they approached. We also piled garbage all around, hoping the stink would keep them away.

My brother Ignaz was an engineer at one of the German factories located inside the ghetto, a Többens shop, I believe, and he had "iron" papers that said, "If you find this man inside the ghetto during the day, don't take him because we need him to run our factory." Once the Germans raided the ghetto during the day and found him on the street, but he showed them his document and they let him go. And another time they let him go. And another time. Then one day, the day before he was to join Joel and me as railroad workers, they caught him and didn't let him go. By this time even "iron" documents didn't mean anything. The SS were only concerned with filling their daily deportation quotas. They sent him to Treblinka with his wife and their beautiful three-year-old son, Kubus, a really special little kid. He was amazingly smart and a wonderful little boy. Even at three years old he understood what was going on. When the Germans were making their raids in the ghetto, no one wanted to have babies or young kids around because they would cry or make a noise and give away your hiding place. This little fellow would go to the adults and talk baby talk to calm them. "Shhh. Don't talk so loud," he'd say. "The Germans might hear you." The Germans murdered all three of them, I assume, at Treblinka.

Resistance

The creation of the ghetto was especially hard on Jews from outside Warsaw. Warsaw Jews had their own homes or knew someone they could stay with, as we knew Uncle Joe, my mother's brother. Not so lucky were those from outside the city, most of whom were poor village people dumped into Warsaw with just the clothes on their backs and a few other possessions. Warsaw Jews took in as many people as they could, but there were still thousands of homeless people on the streets. I shared a single room with my mother, my sister Helen, and my brother Joel and his wife Ala.

How did we learn about the atrocities? How did we learn that the labor camps to which people were being deported were really extermination camps where mass killings were taking place? In my case, it happened like this: Krysia Totenberg was a girlfriend of mine from the Conservatory, a violinist whom I used to accompany on the piano. She lived not far from us, and one day I stopped in to see how she was doing. A few of her relatives were there, including a cousin who had just come from Lublin, where the atrocities began.

He was a fellow about six feet, two inches tall, blond with blue eyes. No one would have suspected he was a Jew. In fact, he didn't even wear a Star of David. He looked like a total Aryan. "The Germans are killing people by the thousands," he told us. "They are burning them, they're gassing them, they're hanging them, they're shooting them. They're murdering them left and right." By then, most of the Jews in the ghetto had already been deported.

I could not believe my ears. "What are you talking about?" I said. "Are you sick or something? Are you sure you're really all right?"

"I'm perfectly fine," he said. "I'm telling you the truth!" None of us wanted to believe him.

Who *could* believe that the Germans could be such a murderous nation? A nation that created great composers such as Bach, Beethoven, and Brahms. Great writers like Schiller and Goethe. Painters. Philosophers. Who would believe they could decide to kill a whole race? Millions of people. It was just crazy and unbelievable, but rumors were circulating.

A few weeks later two fellows from our work group finally convinced me of what was happening. These guys were first-class smugglers, brave and smart enough to risk their lives every day. One morning, for example, they left for work with furs under their winter coats. At the ghetto gate they encountered eight SS men busy searching people. Despite the danger, they passed between two pairs of SS men, acting as if they had already been searched, and then they passed between the next two pairs the same way. If they had been discovered, they would have been shot right there at the gate. That's how much guts they had.

One day to buy things they could sell to the Poles, they stayed in the ghetto instead of going to work. Jews were working at the airport or on the railroads, and there wasn't supposed to be anybody inside the wall except the old, the sick, or children. The Germans made a raid and caught these two guys and we thought, "Well, that's it. They're going to a labor camp. We won't be seeing them again."

The next day our work group was fixing track at Warsaw West when, out of the blue, these same two guys came walking toward us along the tracks. "Where the heck are you coming from?" we asked.

"Shhh! Let's get on the side and talk. We just came back from hell."

The Germans had taken them to Treblinka, a first-class killing factory. They had arrived at night on a train that carried thousands of people. In the glow of bonfires they made out freshly dug mass graves. A group of workers stood around its leader, an SS officer in a white uniform.

The SS officer ordered all the arrivals to disrobe and throw their clothes on a pile. These two guys pretended to undress, and when the naked people were told to start marching, the two guys hid in the huge pile of clothes. When the Germans or some Polish workers, I don't know which, began putting the better clothes back onto the train for shipment to Berlin, these two guys managed to smuggle themselves back into a cattle car. The clothes and belongings taken from the Jews were going to Berlin via Warsaw. There were no longer guards on top of each car, just one guard in the front and maybe one in the back of the thirty or forty cars. In the morning the guys recognized us working on the track and knew they were in Warsaw West, so they jumped off the train.

From what they told us I became completely convinced that the Germans planned to liquidate all Jews. Those of us who heard these two men decided right then that we were going to fight, that we weren't going to be led to our deaths like sheep. But *how* were we going to fight? With what? With our bare hands against the best army in Europe, armed to the teeth? We decided we would try to buy guns.

We had contact with the Polish underground in Warsaw, so we bought some guns from them, paying dearly for each one. The problem was how to smuggle the guns into the ghetto. Since the Germans allowed Jewish workers to bring a two-pound loaf of bread and a few potatoes back with them after work, the Poles baked our guns, along with a few bullets, into bread, and we carried the guns into the ghetto inside the loaves. I brought mine in that way. At the gate when we returned from work the day after we brought in the guns, I heard the German officer in charge yell at the SS men, "The Jews have guns in their bread! Cut the breads!" I don't know how his spies found out about it, but he was one day too late.

We started to build bunkers. Of course, we knew we didn't have a chance against the German army, but at least we would go to our deaths fighting. I wish we had known the Nazi plans when we were five hundred thousand people in the ghetto instead of the remnant that remained. My father and my brother Ignaz and his family had already been taken, and now my mother was also gone, along with my sister Helen and my brother Joel's wife Ala. They had been taken on Monday, January 18, 1943, during the Second *Aktion*, while Joel and I were at work. We were by ourselves now.

Even now I could still have escaped. Professor Drzewiecki had sent word to me that he had a false passport waiting for me. A Colonel Levitsky, a friend of his, who was with the Underground, had come to the railroad, and I gave him a photo I had of myself. Then they made up a document with a false name ending in *ski*. I was to use it to go into hiding in the villa of a prince near Lublin. But I didn't want to leave Joel behind, so I asked that a second passport be made for him. In the meantime, the uprising broke out, and we were trapped.

When they say there was an uprising in the Warsaw Ghetto, what does that mean? There were several separate organized groups, with their central commands, that attacked the Germans, but most people were fighting in isolation. Those who had guns shot back, but it wasn't an organized thing. People formed groups and prepared themselves by building bunkers, but they didn't tell anyone else where it was for the simple reason that when the Germans caught you they'd say, "Do you want to live? Tell us where the other bunkers are, and we'll let you live." If you told them, they would catch the others and then would shoot you anyway. So everyone knew that the safest way was to build your bunker and keep your mouth shut about it.

How and where did we build our bunker? When the Germans first built the wall around the ghetto, it enclosed more than half a million people. Later, when there was less than a tenth of that number left, they built a second wall farther inside the ghetto. The area between the two walls surrounding the few fenced-off factory areas was called *Niemandsland* (No-Man's-Land). We called it the wild ghetto. If you were willing to take a chance and go into No-Man's-Land, you could roam around in any apartment you wanted to. Since no one lived there anymore, the windows were broken, the doors were open, and you could take whatever had been left behind. When you needed wood for a fire, you went into an empty house with an ax and chopped up a closet door or broke up some chairs and carried away the kindling. I got plenty of wood that way. You tried not to think about who had lived there.

I belonged to a group with some well-educated people in it, including engineers. We found a house right next to the inner wall and built a bunker in its basement. But you can't just hole up in a bunker in a basement—you have to be able to go out and see what's going on in the world or find something to eat. You can't just sit there. So our engineers built a tunnel from our basement, under the ghetto wall, and into the basement of a building in the wild ghetto. They cut out the tunnel, brick by brick, and built a little flatbed with wheels. When you wanted to go out, you pulled the little wagon out of the wall and went. Then somebody on the inside pulled it back into place. It fit like a glove. You couldn't see anything from the outside.

We figured that when our building was burning, we would at least be able to escape through the tunnel and maybe survive a few more days. We knew we would eventually be caught, but at least they would not find us suffocated with our guns in our hands. We planned to say we had been roaming around in No-Man's-Land for days looking for food and had nothing to do with the uprising. In the meantime, the women baked *suchary*, a dried bread or hardtack, and stored it in the bunker, along with flour we had bought from the Poles. We also packed mud and dirt around the outside of the building, along with plenty of stinking garbage, so the Germans wouldn't want to come in.

So April 19, 1943, arrived, and the Germans came into the ghetto with all their guns to clean it out, not expecting anything except to be able to kill whomever they wanted to kill. They had sealed off the ghetto in the early morning, and no one had to be told what that meant: a mass roundup and deportation to Treblinka. We watched and waited for them on the roofs. I was on a rooftop right across from where the monument to the Warsaw Ghetto Uprising now stands. How much ammunition did we have? Not much.

When the Germans arrived, we started shooting, and all of a sudden Germans started dropping dead. Maybe they weren't such supermen after all. When they were shot, they didn't just pull the bullet out and throw it away. When they caught a bullet, they fell down just as dead as any Jew.

Caught by surprise, the Germans retreated from the ghetto, and when they came back, they brought their artillery and even bombers. Still, we managed to fight on for about six weeks. We fought back and refused to give up. People jumped out of windows rather than surrender.

Finally, in May 1943, when it came time to escape through the tunnel, we scattered throughout No-Man's-Land. We roamed around there for several days looking for food, sometimes finding stale bread, sometimes a little water. The Germans finally captured Joel and me in No-Man's-Land and took us to the *Umschlagplatz*, the place at the edge of the ghetto where the Germans brought Jews and loaded them onto trains headed for the camps. With the SS and their vicious dogs all over the place to keep order, they marched the uprisers—the last Jews of the Warsaw Ghetto—to the train.

They packed about 120 people into cattle cars big enough to

hold 50 people. My brother, who was marching in front of me, was the 120th. When the SS man put a hand between him and me and told me to stop, Joel instinctively turned around. "You turn around once more," the SS man said, "and I'll kill you." He didn't know that he saved our lives by dividing us. Not that he wanted to. Since Joel was the last one in his car, he ended up next to the small opening with bars, so he was able get some air. People suffocated inside those freight cars, all packed together like cattle. People fainted and died on each other's shoulders. It was so packed there was no place to fall. All kinds of horrible things went on in this hell.

Since I was the first one in the next car, I immediately went to the window on the far side, so I also ended up with air to breathe. Next to me in the cattle car I discovered a younger schoolmate whom I had known at the gymnasium. When the train got rolling, I said to him, "I'm going to jump. I'm not going to let them kill me. My teacher has a false passport waiting for me." I had a razor in my pocket, so I started shaving myself, using saliva on my face. If I was going to try to make it back to Warsaw, I did not want to look suspicious.

About an hour out of Warsaw I heard the two guards above us on the roof of our car talking to each other in Ukrainian. My teacher in Lemberg, Halina Levitzka, who got me the job with the Russian general, was Ukrainian, so I knew a little bit of their language. It's not that different from Polish. I told my young friend that I was going to try to bribe the guards to let us jump. I had two thousand zlotys on me, which wasn't much, but it might be enough. I'd ask them not to shoot us. Maybe it might just work.

I stuck my head out the window and shouted to the guard on the roof. When I got his attention, I said, "Look, I have some money I want to give you. I want to jump. Will you promise you won't kill me?"

"Oh, yeah. Sure."

"Wait a minute," I said. "Not so fast. There's another guard up there with you. It doesn't matter whose bullet hits me."

"Don't worry, I'll take care of it."

"Okay. I have two thousand zlotys. I'll give it to you if you promise not to kill me."

"I give you my word."

"That's not enough," I said. "I want you to lie down on the roof and put your hand down so we can shake on it, and then I'll give you the money." He did and I gave him the money, but in the meantime the people around me were listening to our conversation, and I could tell they were getting agitated.

"The train is going to slow down when it comes to a big curve," he said. "Jump feet first. I'll tell you when. Remember, feet first." I knew he was right about that, so I felt he wasn't lying and that I could trust him. Maybe.

The time was coming for me to jump. The guard had been on this route before, so he knew the spot where the train would slow down. I found out later it was a place near Lublin close to a German military airfield. "Get ready to jump," he shouted. "Remember, feet first. Don't worry, I won't shoot."

As the train started to slow down and go into the curve, all hell broke loose. People started jumping out of the other cars. Rifle fire was cracking all over the place. Some of the jumpers fell down under the train's wheels and had their heads or legs cut off, depending how they fell. There was shooting and screaming going on all over the place.

In the midst of this hell I talked to the guard as fast as I could so he wouldn't shoot us when we jumped. "I had a famous Ukrainian teacher in Lemberg named Halina Levitzka," I said. "Maybe you've heard of her. She was quite wonderful. Remember, there will be two of us jumping, my classmate and myself. I speak Ukrainian well, don't you think? I've known lots of Ukrainians." I was saying anything to make him my ally, my pal, so he wouldn't shoot us.

"Now," he shouted. "Now! Jump now!"

With the help of my classmate I had gotten my feet out the window and was getting set to jump when people inside the car grabbed my shoulders and pulled me back in. Suddenly I was getting kicked and hit.

"What are doing," I shouted. "Are you crazy? Let me go!"

"No. You can't jump. The SS counted how many people they put into this car and now there will be two missing. They'll kill us all."

"Are you mad?" I said. "Where do you think you are going? To a spa? They are going to kill us all anyway. I'm taking my chances." But by now it was too late. While we were having our argument, the train pulled into the military outpost and stopped. That was it for me.

The Germans kept us penned up inside the cars all night without food or water. We were burning with thirst, and some died on their feet, slumped against the shoulders of a neighbor. The metal on the cattle car window became wet from the heat of all our bodies, so I licked the bars for their moisture. I don't think we could feel the horror of it any longer. We were just burned out and numb.

At one point in the night I heard a commotion outside and peered out the window. People were jumping out the windows of their cars and running to a puddle by the side of the track. They had no idea if it was a puddle of water or something left by a horse, but they were so thirsty that they didn't care and were lying down to drink it. Guards came along and hit them with rifle butts. One of the guards shouted, "Anyone who comes out of the cars now will be killed."

When the guards turned away, I thought to myself, "To hell with it! I'll take a chance." Enough morning light had dawned that I could make out piles of clothes nearby and I knew what that meant: the previous transport had come in, the people had undressed, and then they were shot. "Do I have to wait until morning to die?" I asked myself. "Hell, I can get killed now. Why wait?" I jumped down from the car through the little window, ran to the puddle, lay down and drank. I still do not know what it was. I didn't care. It was wet, that's all that counted at that moment. When I looked up, a guard was standing right next to me, pointing his gun at my head. "What did I say?" he demanded.

"Shoot!" I replied. "Who gives a damn? You're going to kill me in the morning anyway. What's the difference? Shoot!" But for some reason he didn't. Instead, he hit me hard with his rifle butt. "Back into the car," he shouted. I ran back to the train, but now the window was too high, and I was too weak to pull myself up. Hands reached out and grabbed my hands and pulled me in.

At daybreak the Germans opened the car doors, and we got out, although not all of us who had entered the cars left them alive. "Raus! Raus! Schnell! [Out! Out! Hurry up!]" They didn't talk, they barked. They sounded just like their dogs. They lined us up into rows, five across. We seemed to be at some sort of camp near the Lublin airport, and we began to see prisoners wearing striped uniforms. At a distance I saw some of them were trying to signal us with hand signs: a finger pointing down meant here, stay here, this is okay; a finger pointing farther up the track, with a sign under the neck, fingers slicing across the throat, meant danger ahead. So I already knew that this was a labor camp, and I'd have to try to stay here because not very far away was a death camp.

I kept ducking through the rows of people looking for my brother, yelling out his name, when I heard the SS calling out, "Schneider! Schuster!" They were looking for shoemakers, for tailors, for barbers, for anybody who might come in handy for them. I saw a famous Warsaw lawyer, Dr. Pryves, and heard him tell the SS he was a tailor. They told him to step out of line, while the rest had to stay in place. So I realized I had to try some sort of bluff like this, but I didn't want to try until I found Joel.

As I was running along the lines of people, looking and calling for Joel, an SS man hit me with his rifle butt. At another point one of their dogs tried to bite me, but I got away. When I finally did find Joel, I said, "Have you seen what's going on here? Do you realize what the Germans want? We've got to stay at this camp and say we're shoemakers or barbers or something." But it was too late. The SS had already gotten their quota of what they wanted. I found out they killed all their Lublin workers two weeks later. They marched the rest of us off to Majdanek.

Part 3:

Inside The Nazi Camps

Majdanek and
Skarzysko Kamienna

Joel and I spent nine weeks in Majdanek in May and June 1943. I couldn't have lasted longer. In another week I would have faded out of this world, dead from hunger and weakness. Majdanek was a huge camp, run by the Waffen-SS of Lublin, with gas chambers and ovens just like Auschwitz. There was a saying there: "The only way to get out of Majdanek is as smoke through the chimney."

The camp was divided into five sections, or fields, four for men and the fifth for women, with rows of numbered barracks on each field. Hundreds of prisoners were packed into each barrack in bunk beds stacked three or more high. Our group was identified as the Warsaw Ghetto uprisers, so the SS gave us "special treatment" in a barrack isolated from others by a high fence—barrack 16, field 3. It quickly became clear they intended to work us to death or just kill us outright.

I still had in my possession my last family photograph—a picture of my mother and father—but my first day at Majdanek they forced us to strip. I folded the photo of my parents and hid it in the palm of my hand as I stood naked, waiting to enter the delousing showers. However, the SS man at the shower entrance noticed that I was holding something. "What do you have there?" he shouted.

"A picture of my parents," I said.

"Give it to me! You don't need it anymore."

He grabbed it from my hand. Ripped it up. Threw it away. I think if ever I was tempted to strangle someone, that was the moment. But I knew not to react, not to show any emotion, not to give them any excuse to kill me. You survived by their rules.

The camp wake-up call was at five in the morning, and whoever wasn't up and off his wooden bunk bed in a second was murdered on the spot. The guards didn't bother to wake you, they just killed you, with a rifle butt to the head or by smashing you with a piece of wood the size of a baseball bat.

From five to seven they made us stand outside the barracks in our striped pajama uniforms to wait for roll call. It might be snowing or raining or sleeting, but we still had to stand outside for the two hours. They just left us out there. To try to stay warm, at least a little bit, a fellow would pair off with someone about his size and rub back to back, like two horses rubbing rumps in the rain. At least it was a way to keep ourselves from freezing.

Each prisoner's ration was a tiny piece of bread, a little bit of soup, and some coffee. I don't know what was in the soup and coffee. It probably came from a sewer. It was hardly enough to keep us alive, but they weren't concerned with nutrition.

The first thing the Germans did was test us to see who could be work slaves and who couldn't. I had to pick up a rock almost as big as myself and run with it about a hundred feet, then put it down, pick up another rock, and run back. Then they put us in rows of five and commanded us to walk. They forced us to walk all day without rest. They wanted to wear us out as soon as they could. They didn't really want us to work—they wanted us to die.

Two wooden gallows were in the center of the camp, and while I was there, there were hangings just about every day. I personally witnessed about ten of them, maybe more. Once when a man was so weak that he couldn't get out of his bunk bed, the SS man accused him of trying to escape! He was too sick to get up, and he was supposed to be trying to run away! The Germans thought it was big joke. They took him to the scaffold and made the man stand on a stool. Then they tied a rope around his neck and kicked the stool away. They made us all stand there and watch him hang. All we could think about was how our soup was getting cold.

There was one man who had real guts. They stood him on the stool and tied the rope around his neck. But then as the SS guy was about to kick the stool away, the man spit on the rat and kicked him hard between the legs—right where it counts. The SS guy doubled up and fell over. He wasn't dead. He just fainted from the pain. Another SS bastard ran up and pulled the stool away, so the man was hanged.

The camp was just one big horror—hell on earth. Of the many thousands of people who died there, about half were killed in the gas chambers or executed, while the other half died from conditions in the camp—starvation, exhaustion, disease, and beatings. They were constantly beating and killing people. Some of the scenes I can't describe and won't even try to, because they're not fit for people to read.

For those who couldn't take it anymore, there was an instant way out. The camp was surrounded by a double barbed-wire fence connected to a high-voltage transmission line. There were watchtowers equipped with searchlights. If you wanted to get shot, all you had to do was get within a few feet of the fence, and they would kill you. Many people took that way out of Majdanek.

Each day I got weaker and weaker. My energy was so low that after coming back from work, I had to hold onto the barrack door handle with both hands and pull myself up the one small step, just a few inches high. And I was twenty-five years old.

About my eighth week at Majdanek a Polish foreman named Antek, also a prisoner, who had befriended me a little bit, said to me, "Marian, you're not going to live much longer. You're just barely alive." He told me he had heard that the Brownshirts, the SA, were supposed to be coming to Majdanek soon to select people to work in armament factories. Thousands of German youths were at the front in Russia, so the German factories needed workers. "So you report," he said. "They might come any day. When you hear the call, run. Get out of here before you're dead."

A few days later I heard the SA were in Majdanek, and I went to my brother as fast as I could: "Joel, the Brownshirts are here. Let's go report."

But my brother had been a little luckier than me, so he wasn't all that eager to leave. He'd gotten a job in the kitchen, peeling potatoes.

"I'm not going," he said.

"What do you mean, you're not going? Why not?"

"Well, I'm sitting here under a roof, aren't I? It doesn't rain on me, nobody beats me, and I eat raw potatoes. How long I live, I'll live. They're going to kill us all anyway. At least I'll have some peace before I die."

So I stayed. I'm from a big family, and I didn't want to go on alone. When Antek saw me the next day, he shouted at me, "What? You're still here? Why didn't you go? You *want* to die here? Listen, you idiot, they're coming again in a few days for a shipment to another camp. If you don't report and get out, I'm going to kill you myself with my own hands. If your brother doesn't want to go, then go without him. He'll die here. Get out of here—you might have a chance. Save yourself."

When the SA came the next time, I went to Joel and put it to him straight. "This place is another Auschwitz. They're going to kill all of us. If you don't come with me this time, I'm going alone.

C'mon!" He took off the apron covering his knees and threw it down. "Okay," he said. "Let's go." So we went and joined about five hundred others who also hoped this might be a way to escape death.

They formed us into close columns of five about a hundred rows long, with the SA and the SS standing together in front. Then the test began, a run of twenty or thirty meters, as fast as we could. Those who fell or couldn't make it were thrown out. Joel and I had become separated, but he was in pretty good condition from working in the kitchen, so I was confident he'd be all right.

I had horribly swollen ankles, but I managed to make those twenty or thirty meters. I didn't break any records, but I made it. That was all that mattered. So I thought I was okay. Nope. An SS man went to the front of the ranks and shouted, "Pull up your pants!" and began physically inspecting prisoners for swollen legs or ankles. Anyone with that condition was thrown out. I thought to myself, "That's it for me."

The SS man worked his way through the columns until he was standing in front of our row. I was in the middle of the row, two guys to my right, two to my left. He was just about to open his mouth and tell us to pull up our pants when another SS man came up behind him and tapped him on the shoulder. The two of them walked a few feet away and began to talk.

I whispered to the man in front of me, "Change with me. I have swollen ankles. They'll throw me out. Your legs are all right. You'll make it again. C'mon! Change!"

"No," he said, "I don't want to. I'm afraid."

I had only a matter of seconds.

The guys around us had heard us. "Idiot! What's the problem? C'mon, change," they said to him. "There's a life to be saved here. If you don't change, *we* will kill you." That scared the hell out of him because he knew they meant it, so we changed places. The moment we switched, maybe a second or two later, the SS man turned around. "Pull up your pants!" he ordered. This fellow pulled up his pants, and he passed again.

That's how I was able to leave Majdanek. I found out after the war that just a few weeks later they sent everyone in barrack 16 to the gas chambers. Smoke through the chimney.

The SA put us on a train and sent us to a former Polish munitions factory in a town called Skarzysko Kamienna. There were many, many buildings there. Mine was called Automats. My job was to cut a part for a machine gun. You cut something in half with a knife to make two parts. I was too weak to understand what it was all about. That's what they told me to do, so that's what I did—and I was very lucky to be doing it.

With my swollen legs and ankles, I could barely walk. I remember the amazement I felt watching others walk around the factory. The latrine could not have been more than twenty-five feet from where I worked, but it took me forever to get there. When I saw people walking normally, without effort, I thought, "God, did I ever walk like that?" I was just about dead.

One night shift—around four in the morning—I fell asleep at my workbench. A German guard came up behind me and hit me hard on the back of my head to "wake" me. My left hand flew forward into the round knife I had been using at my work and cut deeply into my second finger. The cut was nearly a half inch deep, and there was blood all over my hand, but worst of all, it severed half the nerve.

There was a doctor among the prisoners who managed to stop the bleeding, but by then my finger had swollen wider than a piano key. "You'll never be able to play the piano again," he said. "It will remain this wide." But then he had an idea that, thank God, proved his first thought wrong. "Try to get one of the Poles to bring you some *calium hypermaganicum*." These were crystals that could be immersed in hot water to turn the water into a deep blue-purple disinfectant.

Through a Pole I was fortunately able to obtain some of the crystals, so I bathed my finger in the disinfectant as often as I could. Eventually the swelling started to subside. When my finger began to return to normal, I sat down at a wooden table and mimicked playing the piano, hitting the table as if I were depressing piano keys. Thankfully, I felt some feeling at the tip of my finger. You can't imagine what a great relief it was to feel hopeful that I might some day play again. That hope was often all that kept me going.

Conditions gradually got a little better for us, mostly because we began having contact with the outside world. There were civilian Polish workers at Skarzysko Kamienna who went home after work, men who had been employed at the factory when it was Polish owned and continued working there for pay after the Germans took it over. My brother became friendly with one of them and through him was able to get a letter delivered to his German friends in Warsaw, *Volksdeutschen* who were Polonized.

Joel had left his wife's fur coat with them, so he asked them to sell it and send the money to his Skarzysko Kamienna factory friend. His factory friend used the money to buy food and then smuggle it to us. That way we started to eat better, which made all the difference between life and death. Most prisoners were slowly starving.

The Polish factory guys and our guys did business. You could buy bread, a roll, a piece of cheese, a slice of salami. Once I had a little bit of marmalade—I don't remember how I got it. Anyway, marmalade isn't very nutritious, so I sold it for a few *giosze* (Polish pennies). Now I could buy a portion of soup. The Germans gave soup to their Polish workers, so I tried to find a Pole who would sell his to me. In the building where I worked, the Poles were poor, so they ate their portions of soup. But in the next building, a tool factory called Narzendziownia, the Polish toolmakers earned enough money to bring in their own food. They were willing to sell the German slop to whoever paid them for it.

On a lunch break I ran next door with my pennies and asked one of our guys, "Do you know any Pole here who would be willing to sell me his soup?" He pointed to a man in the corner.

"Go over there. He sells his."

When I approached this man and asked if he would sell me his soup, he looked at me strangely. "How come you speak such perfect Polish?" he asked. At that time in Poland most Jews, especially those from small towns, spoke Polish with an accent.

"What do you mean 'how come?' " I said. "I went to school. Didn't you?"

"Okay, okay. Here, eat the soup," he said.

"How much do I owe you?"

"Nothing. Come tomorrow. Come every day." We became friends. It turned out he was the former police commissioner of Skarzysko Kamienna.

Once in a while he would ask me about myself, and we would talk. I told him who I was and what I did and so on. I even told him about Professor Drzewiecki and the false passport he had had made for me. The problem was that my new friend always worked the day shift, while my brother and I worked seven day shifts one week, followed the next week by seven night shifts. So when I saw him for seven days, my brother and I would eat a little better, but then for the next seven days we wouldn't. Then when Monday came around, the cycle started again.

One day he said to me, "I broke my glasses, and I can't get my prescription filled here, so I got a permit to go to Warsaw. Why don't you give me a few words for your teacher at the Conservatory, Professor Drzewiecki? Maybe he'll be able to help you." So I ripped a piece of brown wrapping paper from a machine that was there and I wrote, "This is an honest man. He'll tell you everything about my situation." I signed the nickname my teacher had been calling me since I was a twelve-year-old kid.

Now came the long wait through a week of night shifts before I could see my friend again. I didn't realize how much I longed for news from my old friends in the world. Finally, Monday noon arrived. When the lunch bell rang, I went over to Narzendziownia as fast as I could to talk with him. "Hi! You're back. Did you see my teacher?"

"Don't be in such a hurry," he said. "Eat the soup."

"Never mind about the soup. Did you see him?" He nonchalantly took out a white roll and offered it to me. White bread was a real luxury. "Hey, c'mon," I said. "You don't have to give me something like that. Once in a while I can accept a piece of black bread, but not a white roll!"

Then without saying a word he put a piece of salami on the table and pushed it toward me. Then I realized what was going on. "Uh-oh. That's not from you," I said. "That's from my teacher. You saw him!"

"Uh-huh. I sure did," and he began to tell me what had happened, enjoying himself greatly. "Well, I found his apartment house—a beautiful place in the best part of the city—and knocked on his door. He opened it himself, a fine-looking gentleman. Only he kept the chain on the door. I said, 'I have regards for you from your student, Marian Filar.'"

"'I don't know anybody by that name,' he said. He was afraid, and I don't blame him. He didn't know who I was. So I took out your piece of brown paper and showed it to him through the crack where the door was open on the chain. 'Oh, God!' he said. 'Is he really alive? We thought he was dead. Come in.' Well, I told him everything you had told me, and he gave me a suit for you, a couple of shirts, and a pair of shoes. I'll bring you one shoe tomorrow and the other the day after. And he gave me a few hundred zlotys for you, too."

"Sell the suit," I said. "Don't bother to bring it. The guards will know right away I have contact with the outside. They'll hang me in five minutes. Besides, when am I going to wear a suit in here? Sell it and use the money to bring my brother and me some extra food." So that's what he did. By the way, some of our guys, when they saw me doing business with him, warned me, saying he was a thief who had stolen from the Jews. Maybe he had. Maybe he had not. All I can say is that he was always honest with me, and I confirmed this with Professor Drzewiecki after the war. And he helped save my life by giving me extra food.

Professor Drzewiecki's shoes were a real blessing. Thank God we wore the same size! I had been working with swollen legs and ankles in wooden clogs—Dutch shoes—and I could hardly lift them. I'd just drag my feet along.

There was a barrack of female prisoners at Skarzysko Kamienna, and one of the prisoners from the barrack, a very lovely girl from Vienna, was taking in shirts to wash, drying them on a rope in the sun. Since I now had some money, I gave her my two new shirts to be laundered. A few days later when I came back for them, she said, "Here they are, you pig."

"Pig? Why are you calling me a name? What have I done?"

"Look!" she said, and she showed me two condoms she had found in a shirt pocket.

"Hey, I just got these shirts from the outside," I said. "I know nothing about it. I'm completely innocent. Throw those things away!" After the war I asked Drzewiecki, "Professor, what were you thinking?" But he hadn't known they were there. His maid had simply selected two shirts at random and given them to my friend. Anyway, it was good for a laugh.

Now that friends knew I was still alive, I occasionally began to receive money from the outside, a great help for my brother and myself. Money meant food, and food meant life. Professor Drzewiecki organized private concerts of Chopin's music in Warsaw homes and sent the donations from the concerts to me via my Polish friend. Classmates of mine from the Conservatory played Chopin at these gatherings, something strictly forbidden by the Germans. The Nazis were trying to destroy Poland in every way that mattered, including attempting to destroy people's culture and spirit.

Once I received a really wonderful letter from the mother of a classmate, Marysia Sobol. The former police commissioner slipped it to me during a lunch break, adding that five hundred zlotys had come with it—a lot of money, as good as a million dollars since it would buy bread for quite some time in the camp. Marysia's mother had sent the money.

Joel and I went to the men's latrine, where he stood guard in front of a little cubicle while I read the letter, an absolutely beautiful communication. As I read it, I wept, knowing that I had to tear it up and destroy the pieces so I wouldn't be caught with it.

It so happened that a colleague of mine from the Warsaw Conservatory, Irene Stern, was a foreman at Skarzysko Kamienna because she spoke fluent German. She introduced me to another foreman, who arranged an extra portion of soup for me. And a little extra soup was life. Then I introduced my brother to him, and he too received an extra portion of soup. As I began eating better, I began to feel stronger. Once a couple of black market guys came up to me and said, "Filar, we thought you were going to kick the bucket. Look at you now! You must be getting some money from the outside." I didn't say anything. I just kept my mouth shut.

Then I had a little problem. In the very hot summer of 1943, after I had been in Skarzysko Kamienna for about five weeks, I developed a bad abscess on my rear end. Because of the hundred-degree heat, I had been sleeping naked on a wooden bunk, and a splinter from one of the planks got me. Things like this were life-and-death matters in the camp, a place without doctors, infirmary, or medicine. If you got sick, you died. If you couldn't work, you were killed off—quickly. And I was in a lot of pain.

When things got bad, I went to another prisoner in our barrack with two years of medical studies under his belt who was our "doctor." After his "examination" he volunteered to lance the abscess for me once it softened. "I'll open it up when it gets ripe," he said, "but I have to tell you, I don't have any anesthetic."

When the time came, they tied me to a little table in a barrack selected for the "operation." Four guys held down my arms and legs, with Joel holding my left leg. They wanted to make sure I didn't move. If I jumped when the medical student operated, I could be injured even worse. He took a knife, stuck it in a flame, and when the knife got white hot he came toward me. "Start yelling," he said. "I don't have anything to give you for the pain, and it's going to hurt like hell. So you can start yelling now." And I did. I would have hit the ceiling if I hadn't been held down.

After the operation, I was too weak to go back to work. Besides, the abscess needed time to heal. I had no choice but to go into hiding. I did this by staying one step ahead of the German guards. I hid in a barrack they weren't checking, and when they moved, I moved. During this period, which lasted about a week or so, everyone in my barrack gave me a teaspoon of his soup at night so I could have an extra portion, and this got me back on my feet.

I had to be careful not to be found in the barrack during the day, which would have certainly cost my life. Fortunately, I was able to avoid the camp commander, a Nazi sadist named Kinnemann, a little guy barely five feet tall with a grotesquely large hunchback stuffed inside his uniform. There was a rumor that when he had been the building superintendent of a Jewish old folks home in Leipzig and found someone too sick to get out of his bunk, he'd say, "Oh, this is too bad. Come with me. Come, come, we'll take a little walk outside. The air will do you good." Then when they got a short distance away from the barrack, he'd take out his pistol and murder the poor soul. Soon after the war, and purely by accident, several of my friends from the barrack spotted Kinnemann walking along the tracks near the train station in Ulm, Germany. They grabbed him and paid him back on the spot. They beat him to death and were arrested, but the British MPs let my friends go after hearing why they killed him.

By the time I healed from the operation and returned to work, the weather was changing. Winter was coming, and I knew from experience that I'd better be prepared. Irene introduced me to a Jewish fellow named Tepperman, who was in charge of the camp's clothing magazine, which was stocked with garments from murdered people. I asked Tepperman for a winter coat, and he gave me a pretty nice one. So I said, "How about one for my brother?"

I guess he thought that was asking too much. He went crazy and screamed at me at the top of his lungs. "I don't have anything for your brother! Always 'my brother, my brother!' "

"Always my brother?" I said, "Is that so? Do you think I can walk around wearing a coat in the winter and watch my brother freeze to death? Are you crazy?" I took off the coat and said, "If you haven't anything for my brother, then keep this one too." I gave him back the coat and began walking away. He shouted after me, "Come back here, come back here!" He gave me back the coat and gave me another one for my brother. You didn't try anything on, by the way. He just threw something at you, and you took it. Whether it fit or didn't fit didn't matter. Who cared? Anything to keep from freezing.

Buchenwald and Schlieben

By September 1944 my brother and I had been at Skarzysko Kamienna for fourteen months. Since the Russian front was advancing westward, the Germans began moving their property back out of harm's way. They again packed us into cattle cars, but this time we went just as we were, dressed in our striped prisoner uniforms, with no possessions or marks of personal identity. I remember our train passing through Breslau. It must have been around one o'clock in the afternoon because German kids were coming from school. When they saw us in the cars in our striped clothing, they began throwing stones at us. That's how brainwashed they were.

When we stopped at the train station in Weimar, the birthplace of Goethe, I saw a big sign that said we were eleven kilometers from Buchenwald. There must have been thirty or forty people in our car at that time. "Gentlemen," I announced, "whoever has something to eat better eat it now, because tomorrow we're all going to be dead. We're going to Buchenwald."

As we were waiting in the train at the station, we had a surprise. The SS came knocking on our door like polite businessmen. Since we were going to remain in Germany and they were going back to Poland to bring back more transports, perhaps we'd like to trade some of our Polish money for bread? Well, since I had some money, I bought bread for all of us. So we ate and had a feast, all thirty or forty of us, a feast of bread. The next morning we moved on to Buchenwald, and we all knew what that meant. It was one of the biggest Nazi concentration camps inside Germany, with 130 satellite camps and extension units. It was notorious among prisoners for its slave labor conditions and medical experiments.

In Buchenwald the first thing they did was line us up outside a huge barrack called the *Entlauzung,* or delousing. From a distance the Buchenwald inmates were signaling us with hand signals that the showers were okay. Their message was—"Don't worry. It's going to be water. No gas. No killing." We were munitions workers, and the Germans still needed us.

As we waited outside the *Entlauzung,* I got an idea. If we got through the showers alive, we would need money, and all my money was gone. But Mr. Tepperman, the head of the clothing magazine at Skarzysko Kamienna who came with us on the train, would have money. It was the German practice when they murdered new arrivals to take the better clothing from the murdered and send it to Germany, leaving the stuff they didn't want for distribution inside the camps. Many people sewed money into their clothes or hid coins in the heels of their shoes. I had long assumed Tepperman had collected something. But now that he was going into the *Entlauzung,* where they would strip us of all our clothes, shave our heads, and send us into the showers naked, he wouldn't be able to carry his money into the showers with him. So I told my brother what I was going to do. "I'll ask Tepperman for some money. He knows me. He knows I'm decent. I'll risk taking it in with me, and if I make it, we'll have something to buy food with later."

Joel jumped at me. "Are you nuts? If they catch you, they'll kill you."

"They're going to kill us anyway." I went to Tepperman and put it to him straight. Without hesitating, he handed me the end of a loaf of bread. "There's a ten-dollar gold piece in there," he said—"an American eagle," he called it.

I took it and went back to my brother. "Throw it away," he said. "Throw it away."

"Forget it," I told him. "I'm keeping it." Joel is a pessimist and always has been, while I'm a natural optimist.

Soon we were taken into the *Entlauzung*, a tremendous barrack with bright fluorescent lighting everywhere. There were hundreds and hundreds of prisoners inside, including clergymen and political prisoners from all across Europe. Every sort of language was being spoken.

When they told us to take off all our clothes, I put the ten-dollar gold piece under my tongue and took off all my clothes except my shoes. Then we stepped up to a high table where we were to leave our clothes. When I placed mine on the table, the SS man on the other side said to me, "You've given up everything now?"

Well, I couldn't speak, so I bent down, and with my head under the table out of view I spit the ten-dollar gold piece into my hand. Then I took off one shoe and put it on the table. "Yes, I did," I said. "I already gave everything." I bent down again, put the ten-dollar gold piece back in my mouth, took off the second shoe, and put it on the table. The SS man went on to the next guy. I was completely naked, with the ten-dollar American Eagle under my tongue.

Next we went to a barber to have our heads shaved. I was wearing a small mustache in a style popular in Warsaw at the time, thinking that if I ever escaped it would help me blend in better. That damn mustache nearly cost me my life.

After they shaved our heads, we went to the shower room entrance where another SS man stood guard. As I arrived in front of him, I came to attention. Suddenly he pointed his finger straight at my mouth. For a moment I thought he knew what I had in my mouth and that I had had it. Then it dawned on me that the fool of a barber hadn't shaved off my mustache. That's what the SS man was pointing at.

I came to attention again, turned around, and went back to the barber. I think he was Bulgarian, but who the hell knows? All the nations of Europe were there. I pointed at my mustache, and he shaved it off. Then I went back to the same SS man and stood at attention with the ten-dollar gold piece still in my mouth. "In," he shouted.

So I made it through. But they told one fellow just a few steps behind me to open his mouth, and when they found something, they took him outside and shot him.

A little later I ran into Tepperman. "I got through," I said. "Do you want the coin back?"

"Keep it," he said. "I have enough problems."

Buchenwald was a huge place, with about twenty thousand prisoners in the main camp. They put our group in the tent camp, the *Zeltlager*—no barracks, just big tents with bunks. It was a transit area for people they shipped to armament factories in Germany. Since we were munitions workers and less expendable than others, we were earmarked to go on to another arms factory. They considered us necessary.

The inmates of Buchenwald included many high government officials from France, Italy, and other European countries. Prime Minister Léon Blum of France was there, and Prime Minister Édouard Daladier—quite good company. The SS would arrive in the morning to take roll call and then disappear, leaving the camp administration to the inmates. So the veteran political prisoners ran the camp.

Soon after we arrived, their representatives came to us. "You're going to be here only a few days," they said, "so tell us if you have any collaborators among you. We'll hold a democratic trial, and they'll be sentenced. We won't let them leave with you to drink your blood all over again."

The prisoners accused Tepperman and another fellow by the name of Krzepicki, so a court was set up to try them. Apparently, back in Skarzysko Kamienna they had been policemen and had beaten prisoners, but that had happened before I arrived, so I hadn't seen any of it. When they called me as a witness, I said, "What I'm hearing is horrible, but I must say in Mr. Tepperman's defense that he gave my brother and me winter coats and didn't ask anything from us." Still, the court sentenced him to death, and the other guy too. And that was it for them. I don't know how they were killed exactly, but when it was done their bodies were added to those of others who had died in camp. The SS never knew anything about it. I kept the ten-dollar gold piece, which was worth a small fortune.

While at Buchenwald I wrote a poem about Hitler—in my head, that is. I worked on it line by line while I endured the hell of the camps, and when I was liberated, I wrote it down. If I had written it down in the camp and they had caught me, I would have been hanged in less than a minute. I was only afraid that I might say it in my sleep and that someone would hear me. Anything was possible. All lives hung by a very thin thread. Later, I translated it into English and with some help revised it. I include it now because it reflects my state of mind at the time. It's a very rough translation of the original, which was in Polish and rhymed.

> This is a portrait of you, you "painter," you carbuncle with a mustache, you bandit from Hell.
> You whore, you son of a bitch, you sadist, you sick lunatic—you repository of Evil!
> There are not enough filthy words to describe you. You are a snake born in hell, full of venomous poison, an outcast of the human race!
> You, you mass Murderer, are the symbol of German culture from recent times.
> You push yourself to conquer the world at the expense of millions of innocents.

*You swim in a sea of blood of old people, of women and children, and you
    have the gall to call yourself a hero?*
*Wait, you monster, you gangster. The arm of justice will find you one
    day,*
*And you will pay dearly for all you have done and will not escape your
    destiny.*
You'll go high, very high, all the way to the top of the gallows,
And you will be hanging just like the martyrs today,
*And your nation, which is going crazy about you, seeing their Führer like
    this, will perish with you.*
And you will be robbed of all dignity and self-respect.
You will be looking for pity, a piece of bread, forgiveness,
*And the holy earth will not accept your damned body, it will refuse to
    have you.*
*It will give it away to those horrible ovens which were the highest invention
    of your Reich's culture,*
*And you will burn furiously, horribly, just like your innocent victims
    burned.*
*The fires will consume you and the wind will blow away your despised
    ashes,*
All that will remain afterwards will be a stench and your cursed memory.

The Germans kept us at our tent camp for about ten days before
they shipped us out again, this time to a satellite camp of Buchenwald near Leipzig called Schlieben. The camp was a slave labor
camp for a large factory that produced bazookas and other munitions. My first job at Schlieben was as a *Holzhacker*, chopping logs
and sawing wood for the kitchen—a job I considered myself very
lucky to have. Most of all, I did not have to work on the chemical
vats. That job was a death sentence, and all the prisoners dreaded
it. The factory at Schlieben made a variety of bazooka parts as well
as the chemical mix that went into the heads of bazooka shells.
When a bazooka shell penetrated a tank, the chemicals exploded in
a horrendous fire.

The Germans cooked thousands and thousands of liters of this
yellow chemical mess in immense vats, and prisoners slowly, slowly

stirred the vats with long poles. The Germans who worked there had gas masks, a day off, and special food, but the prisoners got nothing. The fumes coming up from the vats killed you. First your skin turned the same yellow as the chemical, and then you started hacking. Finally, you were too sick to work anymore—and you died. Then they put another prisoner in your place.

Joel was lucky, too. He had graduated from business school in Warsaw, so when the Germans saw that he was better at math and business than anyone they had, they put him in charge of the accounting. He was one smart guy who knew what he was talking about. And Joel was a wise man, as well as a good businessman. In the camps other prisoners always asked him for his advice and opinion about life-and-death matters. People would say, "Go ask the elder Filar." He had quite a reputation.

Besides not having to work the vats, I was also lucky in another way. Polish girls worked in the kitchens. There was a women's barrack at Schlieben, but it was located in a distant corner of the grounds, so the kitchen was the only place where you might see a woman. One day when I was sawing wood, I heard female voices speaking Polish, so I joined right in and spoke Polish with my Warsaw accent. It turned out that one of the girls who worked in the kitchen was from Warsaw. We became friends, and she figured out a way to get me extra food. She worked in the SS dining hall, so she found a way to steal food from the SS and give it to me—good food, real food, not swill like the stuff they doled out to us. She would shove one of the big containers at me and yell, "Wash that out!" and then whisper, "There's food in there." It was great while it lasted.

Our daily rations were minimal. Normally, we would get "soup" at noon and in the evening some coffee—at least that's what they called it—and a piece of bread, and then every other day a little piece of salami or margarine. That was it. Everyone was half dead from starvation. That's why you had to steal food if you wanted to survive. We stole food at every opportunity, even from the railroad station and trains, where our workers stole potatoes, sugar beets, and whatever else they could find. It was the only way to stay alive. But if you were caught, they killed you instantly.

My situation changed for the worse after an act of sabotage on the factory grounds. It happened around two in the morning. I was sleeping on the top tier of a three-tiered bunk bed when all of a sudden there was a tremendous explosion and the whole back wall of our barrack just fell away. My bunk crashed down on the guy below me, and both of us fell onto the guy on the bottom. Luckily, no one in the barrack was seriously hurt.

A storage area that contained hundreds of thousands of tons of ammunition had blown up, and the huge explosion forced the Germans to stop their production of bazookas at Schlieben for two or three months. They suspected all of us, so in retaliation they sent in the young SS to teach us a lesson. These guys were maybe eighteen or nineteen years old and had grown up under Hitler. They were the worst. They clubbed us viciously and shot prisoners left and right without thinking about it twice. They were always threatening to kill people, and many times they did.

As much as they beat and humiliated us, I knew they could not take away my talent, my gifts, my knowledge, my love of music, what I am. To them I was only a number, a slave. They knew nothing about me, which was just as well. Even without a piano I always had music in my heart, which is why I never thought of suicide, no matter how bad things got. Plus, I wouldn't have wanted to give those SS bastards the satisfaction of thinking they had triumphed over me.

When the Germans decided to move some of the heavy machinery to a safer place, I was one of eight men they chose to move it out of the factory and onto freight trains. At least the eight of us knew what we'd be doing for a few months, so that was good—we didn't have to stir the chemical vats. But the machines were incredibly heavy, and we had to move them long distances, sometimes uphill. There weren't carts or horses to help—just the eight of us.

We managed it by laying a track of pipes and rolling the machines along it, then bringing the pipe from the back to the front and repeating this over and over again. But what was worse than the work itself was that I was kept away from the kitchens and my friend. Now our foreman went over to the kitchen and got the exact amount of measly rations for the eight of us.

One day in late 1944, just before Christmas, while we were moving machinery through a forest, our foreman, an inmate by the name of Lopek, came up to me and told me that the chief of the whole camp wanted to see me. The chief was a civilian Hitlerite who wore a swastika on his lapel.

"The chief wants to see me? Are you kidding? What for?"

It turned out the SS had built a little stage in one of the factory halls we were clearing and had decorated it with greenery. They had gotten a piano from some peasant and put it in there for their Christmas show.

"I told the chief we had a concert pianist here," the foreman said. "The chief said, 'Is that so? Bring him here. I want to hear him play.' "

"Are you crazy?" I shouted. "Don't do me these kinds of 'favors.' You know what's going on. You know they're killing Jews with any education."

"Shut up and go. He's waiting."

So I went. I had no choice. If you tried to run away in those striped uniforms, they shot you before you got ten yards. But now I was seriously wondering if my luck had run out. I didn't want to be singled out in any way.

There were about fifteen young German girls in the hall when I walked in, girls about sixteen or seventeen, who were adding the incendiaries to the bazookas in wooden boxes for shipment.

I stood at attention while the chief looked me over. "Spielst du clavier? [Do you play the piano?]" he asked. When the girls heard his question, they circled around us, full of curiosity. I wasn't sure what the foreman had told him, so I told the truth. I had no choice.

If they caught you in a lie, they shot you. Hell, they shot you for any or no reason whatsoever. It didn't matter.

"Yes, I used to play piano. But look at my hands." And I showed him my calluses. I was replying in German, having begun to understand and speak it fairly well.

"Where did you study?"

Again, I had to tell him the truth. "I graduated from Poland's State Conservatory in Lemberg summa cum laude." When I said that, the young girls' eyes nearly popped out of their heads. They were stunned. They couldn't understand it. They had been fed the line that the prisoners were bandits and terrible people. Then why was *he* here? I thought to myself, "It's worth dying just to see the doubt I put in their minds about what Germany is doing to Europe."

The chief asked, "Do you know Beethoven's 'Moonlight Sonata'?"

"Yes."

"Do you play it?"

"Look at my hands—look at the calluses."

"Do you want to play it or not?"

"Yes, sir. Of course." I sat down at that beat-up old jalopy of a piano, with only one pedal and some keys that didn't come back up, and played the first movement of Beethoven's "Moonlight Sonata." When I finished, the chief asked, "Do you know Liszt's Second Rhapsody?"

My God! Now I knew I was dealing with a sadist! I had barely touched the piano in almost five years. Who can play the Second Rhapsody with callused fingers and a rusty technique? But before the Second Rhapsody becomes fast and difficult, its beginning is broad and slow. So I played it *very* slowly, wondering what I was going to do. I was just reaching the end of that slow section when a German came up to the chief with some important business, and the two of them walked away. Nothing more came of it. I was dismissed and went back to my work. But in the long run that little "audition" saved my life.

A few weeks later something happened that got me thinking about prejudice and racial hatred. At one point several of us were talking, including the German prisoner who was the leader of the barrack, responsible for keeping count of the prisoners and for going to the kitchens to get everyone their rations of soup and bread—the miserable so-called food. He was a Social Democrat whom the Nazis arrested in 1933 when Hitler came to power, so he had been in Nazi camps for twelve years, ten years longer than I had.

It was the beginning of 1945, and we already sensed that the war was changing. I don't know how we knew. They certainly didn't deliver the *New York Times* to the gates. It's possible that the block leader had picked something up from the Germans since he was German. He said to us, "If God grants that we survive this, you people will all go back to your homes. You'll go back to Poland, you to Czechoslovakia, you to Italy. You'll go back to Scandinavia, you to Greece." We were prisoners from every corner of Europe. "But where will I go? My home is seventy-five miles from here. The world is going to blame the Germans—and rightly so—for everything that's happened, and I will be accused all over again. I've spent the war in this hellhole, but the Allies won't know what the Nazis did to me. I'll be just another 'goddamned German.' You'll be free, and I'll be blamed."

That got me thinking. "He's right," I said to myself. "If God does grant that I survive this horror, and I meet a German, I'll first make sure if he's a Nazi before I say anything against him. He could very well be a friend, another inmate—this particular man is a German and he *is* my friend, an ally." He was suffering the same way I was—perhaps a little less. I don't think they beat him up as much or as viciously. Let's just say I didn't see them beating him. As a German, he knew how to talk to them, and of course he wasn't a member of an "inferior race."

Liberation

As our work moving machinery was coming to an end, the eight of us worried that they might make us stir the chemical vats next. It was everyone's nightmare. It meant death. The fact that we looked a bit stronger than many other prisoners didn't help our chances of avoiding the vats.

How did we come to look stronger? Some of the armament machinery was being stored in farmers' barns nearby, so when we went to their barns, we'd engage the farmers in trade. We'd exchange a few shirts we got from the camp clothing magazine for food and then split the food fifty-fifty with the guy in charge of the magazine. So we frequently had a little extra to eat.

One day during our "lunch break," one of our work group announced he had arranged a future job for himself. He had gone to the camp fire department and lied about having been a fireman. So, when our job moving machinery was over, he'd be working at the camp's fire station. No chemical vats for him! I thought to myself,

"This is a smart fellow! He just saved his life. I've got to figure out something like that."

A few days later I was walking on the camp's main street—it was a huge place, as big as a city—when I saw the chief. I said to myself, "It's now or never." I went up to him and stood at attention before him. "Sir, do you remember me? I played the piano for you a couple of weeks ago."

He looked me over. "Yeah, yeah, yeah. What do you want?"

"Sir, should I survive the war, I'd like to go on playing the piano. Otherwise, I have no reason to live. My whole family is already murdered. Would you find me a job where I could save my hands?" While I said this, I looked him straight in the eyes.

He thought for a moment while I stood there—one of the longest moments of my life. "Tell your boss to come to my office," he finally said. I ran as fast as I could to my boss and told him the chief was waiting for him. At first he didn't believe me, but then he went off to see if I was telling the truth. I knew he wouldn't say anything bad about me. A short time later he returned and told me that now it was my turn to go see the chief. When I went into his office, he said, "I've spoken with Mr. Ställer, the head of the *Schiessplatz*. Go see him."

The *Schiessplatz* was a proving ground where they tested bazookas, antiaircraft guns, and all sorts of small-caliber ammunition. It was a huge, sort of mysterious area where shooting went on day and night. I wasn't sure if I might not be entering the site of my own death.

I went to Mr. Ställer's compound and walked into his office. I was trembling, only too aware that I didn't know anything about this Mr. Ställer. He might be an SS man or a Nazi zealot. These guys could do anything they wanted to you, any time they wanted to do it. They had the power of life and death, and there was no accounting to anybody.

Inside the office a tall, good-looking German was standing in a

My first public concert at the Warsaw Conservatory at age six

Newspaper photo at the time of my debut with the Warsaw Philharmonic at age twelve

My teacher, Professor Zbigniew Drzewiecki

Prof. Zbigniew Drzewiecki and Dr. Prof. Stefania Lobaczewska in Lemberg. Both saved me from the Hitlerites.

*Passport photo of my
murdered father*

*Passport photo of my
murdered mother*

*Passport photo of my
brother Michael, who
spent the first part of
the war in Siberia*

*My very dear sister
Helen and my first
piano teacher. She
was beaten and later
killed by the Nazis.*

*My sister Lucy who was
also in Siberia. After the
war she lived in Israel.*

With my cousin, Anne Serko, who was murdered in the Holocaust

With my mother in our apartment before the war

Ernst Ställer, the German who helped save my life— and my hands

Since I had already thrown my uniform away, I had to borrow this larger one for a "souvenir" photo a few days after liberation. I weighed about 80 pounds.

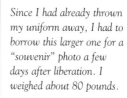

Photo of Nazi SS guards in the last camp I was in. They left it behind after they fled shortly before liberation.

Playing the piano in the D.P. camp outside Frankfurt

Walter Gieseking, the great
German pianist and my teacher
from late 1945 to early 1950

Sol Hurok checking me out

My German 7' 5"
Steinway grand
piano arrived in
New York shortly
after I did in 1950.

*With Eugene Ormandy,
conductor of the
Philadelphia Orchestra*

*Photo of Arthur Rubinstein with inscription
translated from Polish: "To Marian Filar, a
magnificent artist with a warm token of
friendship. New York. 7th April, 1967"*

*Banner announcing
my upcoming concert
appearance in Brazil*

*With my students
at the Settlement
Music School in
Philadelphia*

My brother George (first row, right), who emigrated to Palestine in 1935. He is shown here with his British special commando unit in World War II.

With my brothers at Joel's second wedding in 1959. The Nazis killed his first wife, together with my mother and sister Helen. Shown here left to right: Joel's wife, Nadia, Joel, Michael, and myself.

Each year on May 8, the anniversary of the Allied victory in Europe, I go downtown in Philadelphia and touch the Liberty Bell.

The great violinist Henryk Szeryng rehearsing with his accompanist in my apartment before a concert in Philadelphia. He and I (both at age ten) gave a mutual concert at the Warsaw State Conservatory of Music in 1927.

With colleagues at my retirement party given by the Temple University College of Music in May 1987. Our wonderful dean, Dr. David L. Stone, is on the right.

In 1992 I am in front of the Warsaw Ghetto Uprising Monument about 150 feet from where I was born.

long leather coat. Next to him a pretty secretary was working at her typewriter. Nobody else. When the tall German saw me enter, he greeted me with a friendly "Hello" and thrust his hand out for me to shake. I nearly fell over with astonishment and relief. It was the first decent greeting I had experienced from a German in five years.

"Are you a concert pianist?" he asked.

"Yes. I was just starting my career when the war broke out."

"What pigs!" he said. "I hate those bastards! The world will do plenty to us when this is over, but you've just won your life. You'll stay here and work for me until the end of the war, and you won't lose a hair from your head. What can I do for you?" He actually invited me to sit down on a chair. Unbelievable.

I did a little fast thinking. "Sir," I said, "as far as food is concerned, if I could be a foreman somehow, maybe even my own foreman. That way I could get to the camp kitchen regularly. I know some Polish girls there, and I'm sure I could manage to get some extra food for myself." I was thinking "foreman" because the foreman went to the kitchen with the soup order and then brought it back to his command. "Otherwise, I'll just get my regular portion of soup and that will be it. If I can go to the kitchen myself, my friend will fix me up, and it will make all the difference in the world."

"Okay," he said, "No problem. Let's go set it up. We'll walk over to the gate where they have the bookkeeping and take care of it. But I'm going to have to insult you on the way. I have to do it to keep the Nazis happy. Don't worry about it. Laugh it off." So as we walked over, he yelled at me, "You dirty this, you lousy that! I'm going to shoot you!"

We went to the camp's main gatehouse, where groups were constantly coming and going between the barracks and the factory and standing at the gate to be counted. A SS sergeant was there and one of our guys, wearing an armband with *Schreiber* on it. That meant he was a writer, or more precisely, an accountant. It was his job to keep track of the groups going out in the morning and coming back after work. At Schlieben there were commands of up to four hundred prisoners, each with one or more foremen. The east side of the proving grounds where I would be had a ten-person command.

Ställer told the sergeant, "They sent me this fellow here to work around the office. How's it going to be for his food?"

"Well, you've got ten men on the east side of the proving grounds," the sergeant said, "so he can join 'em and be eleven. That's all there is to it."

"I don't think so," said Mr. Ställer.

"Who the hell are you to tell me if it can or can't be?" barked the sergeant. Ställer was a civilian.

"You don't understand," Ställer said. "He's the only prisoner in our compound. Sometimes we have lunch at noon, sometimes at one. Sometimes we don't have lunch at all, we have so much work. So what do you want us to do? Because a prisoner has to have lunch, we have to stop working?"

When I was sure the sergeant wasn't noticing me, I looked over at our guy and gestured to him, "Come on, say something, say something." The *Schreiber* picked up on it and said to the sergeant, "What can we do? He's got a point."

"How about a command of one person?" suggested Mr. Ställer.

"A command of *one* person?" the SS man shouted. "Are you crazy?"

"I don't give a damn about it," Mr. Ställer said. "What's the difference?"

"Okay! Okay!"

So the sergeant put in his book that I was a "command of one person." That meant that after morning roll call I went all by myself to the gatehouse and reported: "Command of the Proving Grounds Compound reporting, one person."

The SS working at the gatehouse even made jokes about me. They'd see me coming and say, "Look at this! It's amazing! His command is always full. No one is ever missing. The guy in front is always in line, the guys to the side are in line, everyone's in perfect step! Now get the hell out of here!"

So I went to work and returned from work all by myself. It was fantastic! For a while I even got Sunday off. Mr. Ställer did not work on Sunday, so I just stayed in the barracks. But the Germans caught me and knocked me around pretty good. When I told Ställer about it, he said, "Okay, we'll put you to work. We'll leave a broom out for you. Come in at eight in the morning on Sundays and pretend to clean the office, or just sit in a chair and sleep—whatever you want."

The rest of the week my job was to sit by myself in a small room, perhaps twenty feet underground, and raise and lower target sheets for the marksman above me named Walter who was testing ammunition. There was an SS guard outside, but no one could come in except Mr. Ställer. I had an electric heater for warmth and a telephone to inform Walter if he was shooting too far left or too far right. When Walter wasn't shooting, I didn't have to do anything, so I sometimes took a little nap.

My brother was working in a nearby bunker keeping track of ammunition, so occasionally we managed to eat lunch together. Now and then I got hold of some of the oatmeal that our guys stole from the trains, but since I was not allowed to cook, Walter would cook it for me. It was pretty good.

Mr. Ställer visited me each time he received his food rations. He would pull out a three-pound military loaf of bread from under his long leather coat, take out his pocketknife, and cut the bread in half. "Half for you, and half for me," he would say. It was unbelievable! We became real friends.

In Schlieben there were also Italian prisoners of war, a really great bunch of guys. Every morning you could hear them from far away singing opera on their way to work—good singing, too. The Italians had a special status and were free to go out of the camp and come back, so they would have dates with German girls, who were giving them food. The girls loved the swaggering "Italianos" and used to run after them, I can tell you!

I became very good friends with one of the Italian prisoners whose father was a wine merchant. He told me his address once and said, "In case you survive, I want you to visit us." We spoke together even though I didn't know Italian and he didn't know German. Somehow we managed to communicate using only one word, *kucken,* which means "to look." I would say to him, "You *kucken* bread, I *kucken* potatoes," or something like that, and whatever we found we split half and half. I forgot his address, which I'm sick about, but I didn't have a pocket or anything else to keep a note in.

Once the Germans caught one of the Italian workers sleeping in a freight car, so they dragged him out and were going to shoot him. But the rest of the Italians begged and begged and begged, and finally the SS let him live. After the Germans went away, his comrades really let him have it. "You stupid SOB," they told him. "They would have shot you if everybody hadn't begged for your life. *Stupido! Stupido!*" On and on. Every name they could think of! And they knew plenty.

After the Italians got to know me and found out that I was a pianist, they wanted to hear me play. Somehow they cajoled a civilian where I worked named Meister Jan to let us go to a palace outside of the camp that had a piano. As we all marched out the gate, Jan told the guard, "It's okay, we'll be right back. Don't worry about it!" I got to a piano and played for them. What a scene! I was playing *Tosca* while they all sang away at the top of their voices. We had a ball! Then they all crowded around me and were clapping me on the shoulder, "Molto bene, molto bene!" They really were a great group of guys, and how they loved music!

Towards the end of my imprisonment at Schlieben, an SS man stationed as a guard gestured to me to come over to him.

"Me?"

"Yeah. Come here. Don't be afraid. Listen, the war is coming to an end." I heard the implication in his voice: Germany has lost. "I see you are a smart fellow. Get ten guys together and bring them here, and we'll walk away together. What I'll do is escort you to the Americans, see? I'll save your lives. Then you tell the Americans I saved your life, and you'll save mine. Is it a deal?"

"Of course." What else could I say? If I had said no, I would have had something on him, and he would have killed me. Or it could have been a trick. After that, I avoided him like the plague. Whenever I saw him, I went the other way and disappeared into my room in the bunker and laid low.

The guy whose job I took in the bunker was an eighteen-year-old German Hitlerite named Paul. He had quit because he didn't want to sit in that little room in the basement anymore, but he was still around. Mr. Ställer warned me, "This guy is a Gestapo agent. Stay away from him!"

When Paul saw that Ställer liked me, he began picking on me. One day he brought me a sack and said, "That's for you." It was filled with sugar beets that some of our guys had stolen.

I looked at it and said, "What is this? Where did you get it?"

"What business is it of yours where I got it?"

Whoa, hold on! I needed time to figure it all out. So, I said, "You took this away from our guys, and now you want me to take it? Suppose you were in my shoes—would you take it?"

He yelled, "You think too much! Here's something to eat, now eat!"

"Wait a minute, wait a minute," I said. "Suppose it were the other way around, and you were the prisoner. If I gave it to you, would you take it?"

"You philosophize too much!" he said, getting angry.

I gave it back to him and said, "Thank you very much just the same."

I found out later that when the Russians arrived, the Germans denounced Paul, and the Russians sent him off to Siberia, where he probably died. Even the Germans were afraid of him and didn't want him around. He was one of those kids who grew up under Hitler and didn't know any better, a person totally brainwashed by the system, like those girls who surrounded me when I said I was a pianist, or the schoolkids who threw stones at us and shouted "Juden! Juden!" as we were transported from camp to camp.

Later the Germans began putting Schlieben prisoners on trains headed east. The train they put me on took us to a locomotive factory in Bautzen, near the Czechoslovak border, where we stayed a day or two, and then we had to walk. The Germans sent us on a forced march, later called a death march, out of Germany proper to the Sudetenland in Czechoslovakia. We marched twenty-two hours a day without rest, and then they had us sit on the side of the road for two hours. On the march, which lasted almost two weeks, many prisoners died along the way. Those who couldn't go on, who developed a bad foot or something, they shot.

I remember one morning when we were in very hilly country, barely walking because we were all dead tired, the SS captain of our group of a hundred or so prisoners said, "Whoever cannot walk, get on the cart, and you'll ride." There was a horse-drawn cart following along behind us. One of our guys, a young fellow bothered by tight shoes or something of that sort, got into the cart. The rest of us continued walking.

Toward the middle of the day we heard shooting behind us. A minute later this same young fellow came running up, huffing and puffing, all out of breath, and fell in right next to me.

"What the hell happened?" I asked.

"I just escaped being machine-gunned," he said. "When the cart became full, they drove it behind that little hill up there and began unloading. I saw them uncover their repeater guns, so I took off running. They're slaughtering everyone up there!" He zigzagged down the hill with bullets flying all around him, and now he was standing next to me. That made me very nervous, because in this insane atmosphere anything could happen and frequently did. The SS captain could easily make a mistake, think I was the one who had escaped, and shoot me without warning. In a few minutes the captain came striding up to us and pulled the guy out of line. "You can walk now?" he asked, a slight ironic smile on his face.

"Oh, I'm perfectly fine, sir," the fellow said. "No problem." The captain let him live.

Finally, in early 1945 we arrived in the Sudetenland at a place called Miculasovice, which the Germans called Nixdorf. They put us in a small camp just outside Nixdorf that had formerly housed civilian workers from France. Since they had been civilians, there were no fences around the camp, although for us SS guards were stationed at every window and door. About twenty-five or thirty people slept in each room. My brother Joel and I slept on the floor under a table. When one person would roll over, everyone would roll over.

We dug ditches all day long—ditches against American tanks that were expected to come from the west. The German mayor of the town was so grateful for our "help" in protecting his people from the Americans that one day he sent over some special soup as a gift. However, the gift ended up making us go to the latrine so much during the night that the SS thought we were staging an escape. When they threatened to shoot us unless we stopped running to the latrine, one of our guys said, "Look, it's not us, it's that damn soup. We *have* to go the latrine. If you don't let us, the barracks will float away!"

Sometime toward the beginning of May 1945 a little German boy about ten years old came around as we were digging ditches. He looked at me out of the corner of his eye and then made signs that he wanted to give me something. Finally, he opened up his coat and showed me what he was hiding—a German newspaper.

There was a pile of logs right next to our ditch, so when the guard walked away, I said to the boy, "Shove it between the logs and take off." He left the paper and ran. We didn't know what to do with it. Was it a provocation or some kind of a trap? Later, I grabbed the paper and put it under my jacket. After we returned to our barrack, I took it out. It was dated May 2, 1945, and on the front page, in large type, was this headline: "Berlin Falls. Russians Enter the City." The German kid wanted us to know the good news! Can you believe it? A little ten-year-old kid walking around with a newspaper like that under his coat!

On May 7, 1945, the Gestapo chief of the entire Sudetenland visited our camp to harangue us. He was an elephantine man, well over six feet tall and weighing maybe three hundred pounds. He stood in front of our barrack in his resplendent uniform, spitting and swearing at us in German and insulting us with the most vicious names imaginable. At one point he made a solemn vow that he was going to see that all of us were killed.

The next morning at daybreak, something seemed different when I left the barrack to go to the latrine. The guards didn't look the same, but I did not want to stare at them for fear of getting shot. When I returned, I told my brother I thought the SS had gone. Joel went out to take a look for himself. "Yes," he said when he came back, "they're just old men out there—but don't tell anyone yet. We'll all start hopping around from happiness, and those old guys might get scared and begin shooting."

We found out after liberation that the Gestapo chief's vow to have us all killed had been no idle threat. In fact, the SS had set up machine guns in a nearby forest where we were all supposed to have been shot at two in the morning. But at eleven o'clock that night news came that there had been a breakthrough on the eastern front. So the SS and Gestapo ran away and left the camp to be guarded by the *Volksturm*, old Germans in their seventies and eighties whom Hitler had mobilized during the last gasps of the Third Reich. Most of them could barely lift a rifle.

When we opened the windows that morning, these old geezers were there smiling at us. "The war is over," they said. "The Americans will be here soon. You have nothing to worry about. You survived." Then a short time later they disappeared. It was May 8, 1945, V-E Day.

After the liberation we found the German boy who had brought us the newspaper and made him our mascot. He joined us, and we fed him and saw that he was taken care of. When we asked him why he wanted us to know that Berlin fell, he told us the Gestapo had taken his father, a Social Democrat, to a concentration camp, where he died.

Part 4:

After the Storm

The Tables Are Turned

The liberators of Nixdorf were not Americans arriving from the west but units of the Free Polish Army advancing from the east with the Soviet Red Army not far away. Now suddenly the tables were turned. Barracks for the slaves of the Third Reich now became barracks holding Germans. Polish infantry went door to door looking for Nazis. If they saw a sign on a door, written in Polish, saying something like "Please do not disturb. Former prisoners of war here," they moved on. But if a door was without such a sign in Polish, they broke it down and took "war reparations" on the spot. The Poles paid the Germans back in spades for what they had done to Poland and beat the hell out of quite a few of them.

My brother and I were assigned to a little two-story house a half block from the camp. The owner, an old widow whose husband had been killed in World War I, had no choice in the matter. In fact, she didn't even know we were coming. When I knocked on the door, she answered trembling with fright. "Calm yourself," I told her. "We aren't here to kill you. We're decent human beings, not the bandits the SS told you we were. They are the scum, not us. Look, we have to live somewhere, so just give us a room to stay in. We may even be able to share some of the food that the Polish army gives us." We treated her well and put a sign on her door in Polish so nobody bothered her. After a while she even cooked for us, which she didn't have to do. All in all, things were cordial between us.

The day after we moved in with the widow, a friend and I went to search for a piano so I could test my finger to see if there was permanent damage. We came upon a prosperous-looking house where the chances were good we would find a piano, so we knocked on the door. The German man who answered was terrified and shaking. He was sure we were there to take revenge on him. These people knew what had been going on in the camp, although they lied and said that they didn't know, and they knew they deserved to be treated like criminals.

Looking past the man, I saw an upright piano at the end of the hall. "Hey, relax," I said. "Don't be so afraid. We aren't here to kill you. I'm sorry to have to bother you. It's just that I am a pianist, and my finger was injured in the camps. May I play your piano for a few minutes to test my finger?"

"Oh, sure," he said with relief. "C'mon in."

I went down the hall and opened up the piano. I played a few of the keys, lightly pressing them down with my injured finger to see how it felt. Thank God, I could tell I would be able to play again. I still have the scar from the cut, but the tip of the finger was fine, so it didn't become a problem.

As I got up to leave, the German was cordiality itself. "No, no, don't go," he said. "Please remain and play something more." I wasn't yet ready to socialize with a German, so we left.

Next we walked over to the office of the mayor of Nixdorf to ask if there happened to be a piano around that I could use for practice. He handed me the keys to the palazzo that the SS had used, so we went there. When I entered its magnificent ballroom, I discovered a beautiful concert-size grand piano made in Vienna. I almost cried when I saw it.

So I sat down and started to practice. I played a scale, but my arms hurt like the devil was in them. All the physical work I had been doing had taken its toll. Thank God, Professor Drzewiecki had taught me the proper way to handle such a situation. The first day I played ten minutes and quit. The next day I played for twenty minutes, then thirty minutes, then twice a day, and so on. I reviewed the Chopin E Minor Piano Concerto from memory since I had not seen the music in five years.

The man in charge of the Polish army contingent in Nixdorf was a twenty-five-year-old lieutenant from Lemberg named Ted. Since Ted didn't know a word of German, I acted as his interpreter. Just a few days after liberation, around noon, Joel and I were sitting in the old lady's kitchen having lunch when a Polish sergeant bicycled up to the house. "C'mon," he said, "we caught the chief of the Gestapo." I almost choked on my soup when I heard that. "He's in the guardhouse. Let's go. The lieutenant is waiting."

I pushed myself away from the table, and we went to the guardhouse as fast as we could. There he was all right, sitting in a chair and looking down at the floor like a frightened dog with his tail between his legs. He wasn't so resplendent anymore. Now he was in civilian clothes, and he looked like a big nothing. Just a couple of days before he had been strutting around, playing the big man, puffed up with arrogance and pride, threatening to murder us all, and now here he was whimpering like a baby. Ted was standing in front of him with a whip in his hand. Who would have believed this turn of events? The theater couldn't create anything better.

"That's him, Ted," I said. "That's the bastard! How did you get him?"

"Oh, the Germans make wonderful collaborators. They came in here telling me, 'You're picking on the little fish. Why don't you pick on the big one?' 'Like who?' I asked. 'Like the chief of the Gestapo for all the Sudetenland.' "

The German townspeople gave Ted the home address of the Gestapo chief, and Polish soldiers in two jeeps went over and brought him in. And there he sat before us, a coward trembling with fear in his civilian clothes, no longer protected by his fancy uniform and what it stood for. Even sitting in the chair, he was taller than Ted, but now his teeth were clicking so loudly they sounded like casta-nets.

I have to admit, we did give him a little beating, Teddy and I. Not so little, actually. We played kickball with him, and he was the ball. When he lost consciousness, the sergeant poured water on him so he would come to and not miss any of the fun.

Finally, I said to Ted, "Look, that's enough. You're supposed to get some information out of him."

"Okay, when he comes to, ask him for the names of Gestapo and SS members around here."

I should mention that the Russian army, while not in Nixdorf, was operating not far away, and they had put up signs saying, "All SS and Gestapo are to be turned over to us." But Ted had his own idea about that. He said, "We'll take care of them ourselves."

When the Gestapo chief came to, he started talking, and, boy, did he talk! I thought maybe he would refuse to inform on his col-leagues, but he was a coward through and through. Everything he knew he told us—names and addresses, everything he could think of. He spilled it out so fast I couldn't keep up with him. "Hey, shut up a minute," I said to him at one point. "I can't write that fast."

When we finished pumping everything out of him, Ted told him, "Okay, let's go outside." He was ready to kill the guy. The Gestapo chief fell to his knees and begged us with shaking, folded hands to let him live.

I was outraged. "You want to live?" I said. "You? You're a mur-derer. How many hundreds of people have you killed? *You* want to live? You should never have been born, you scum."

Ted gave me his gun. "They killed your parents, Marian. Go ahead, bump him off. Shoot him."

I thought about it for a moment. "No," I said. "I can't do it."

"Why? Are you a coward?"

"No, I'm not a coward," I said. "And I'm not a murderer, either. If he jumps at me I can shoot him in self-defense, but I won't shoot somebody in cold blood."

All the while the Gestapo chief was kneeling there, begging, "Please let me live. Let me live!"

"Shut up!" Ted told him. The sergeant took out his gun and finished him off.

Across from where Joel and I lived were two German women, refugees from Bautzen, who told me they loved music. After they came to the palazzo several times to hear me play, they broached the real subject that was on their minds: would I escort them and their valuables back to Bautzen, now in Polish hands, where they owned a big jewelry store? The Russians had announced that refugees must return to their homes, but the women were afraid to go by themselves. Travel at that time was pretty dangerous since authority over the area was still uncertain. They said that my knowing Russian, Polish, and German would help get them through.

Of course, we would be subject to danger on the way. I was hesitant to go, but they promised me a motorcycle that had belonged to the husband of one of them, a raincoat, some clothing, and watches for Joel and myself. Since my brother and I had nothing to restart our lives, absolutely nothing at all, I finally told them I'd do it.

So we started off the next morning, the two women pushing a small two-wheeled cart and me riding a bike behind them. We were making our way down a small road near a forest when a Polish soldier with a rifle in his hand stepped out from behind some trees. "Hey, where do you think you're going?"

"These are decent people," I said in Polish. "They're okay. Let 'em be." He let us go on, never touching the women or opening their suitcases. After we got past the soldier, the women got the bright idea of tying their suitcases to the panniers on my bicycle. "Nobody's going to search you," they said. That was absurd, of course. If robbers stopped us, they'd check me too, that was for sure.

Anyway, I took the suitcases, and when we moved on into the hilly country, I had to pedal hard because of their weight.

As I pedaled on, I began thinking to myself, "Probably half the things in these suitcases are stolen. Some of it could be my mother's jewelry. Why the hell don't I just turn around when I get to the top of the next hill and leave them? I can coast back home and never see them again." That was one voice inside my head, but another voice said, "No. You never did anything like that before the war, and you're not going to do it now. You take them home." And I did.

Since it was already dark when we arrived, the sisters asked me to stay overnight. They showed me into a little room on the second floor with framed photos everywhere. That's when I almost became sorry I hadn't taken that U-turn. The photos were of one woman's husband in the uniform of the local police, the kind of police that had been doing lots of the killing. Most of that jewelry probably *had* been stolen from innocent people!

In the morning they opened one suitcase in my presence, and my eyes nearly popped out of my head. It was full, whether of diamonds or glass, I'll never know, just as I'll never know where it came from. They gave me a couple of ties, a raincoat, a pair of trousers, two cheap watches, and a pin for my tie. A real pearl pin, they said, so I'd look elegant. I found out later it was a fake. They offered me the motorcycle, but since gas wasn't available, it would have been a worthless hindrance, so I didn't accept it. I rode back to Nixdorf on the bike. When I arrived, some of the fellows blamed me for not having gotten more for my troubles. Okay, so I hadn't been a businessman, but I hadn't been a thief either.

After about two weeks in Nixdorf, we decided it was time to move on. When Joel and I learned there were facilities for refugees in Prague, we decided to go there. Before we left, the mayor of Nixdorf gave us a little document stating that we had been "political prisoners" at the camp there. In fact, we had been slaves slated for extermination after we were no longer useful. I still have that little document.

Searching for Pieces of The Past

The citizens of Prague were wonderful to the thousands of refugees arriving at the city gates. These people also had just been liberated, so the city's spirits were high. They put us up in a large, very clean hotel in the center of the city and provided us with food stamps and streetcar stamps so we could eat and travel around Prague for free. The first thing I did after we settled in was go to the Conservatory of Music, where they let me use a piano studio, so once again I began to practice my beloved art.

One day when I had been in Prague a short while, a friend and I were walking by a beautiful building in the center of the city when we noticed a poster announcing an upcoming performance by the Prague Philharmonic Orchestra. How delighted I was to come upon a concert hall and symphony orchestra after so many years! Since the Polish and Czech languages are quite similar, I was able to learn from a tall uniformed doorman in front of the concert hall that a rehearsal was in progress.

"Who's conducting?" I asked.

"Kubelik."

"Kubelik's not a conductor," I said. "Kubelik was a violinist—one of the greatest—but he's dead, I believe."

"That's right, Jan Kubelik is dead. But his son, Rafael, isn't, and he's the conductor. He's also a great pianist." I did not know any of this, but then the Germans didn't provide us with radios.

When we walked in, the orchestra was rehearsing Dvorak's Symphony from the New World. After about ten minutes my friend said to me, "Okay, let's go."

"You go. I'm staying." I was finally inside a concert hall again, and I did not want to leave without doing something that would help me restart my life in music. When the rehearsal ended, I got up my courage and went backstage. I found Rafael Kubelik and introduced myself. I blurted out that I was a concert pianist, that I had just been liberated, that I had been in the camps for two years, and that I had hardly seen a piano for three years before that. Despite everything, I told him, I had been practicing whenever I could since being liberated and would like to play for him. When I said, "My teacher was Professor Zbigniew Drzewiecki," that did it.

"Professor Drzewiecki? A wonderful man! Of course I'd like to hear you play. But not here. Look at our pianos. They're still on their sides with their legs off. We've just been liberated ourselves, you know. The Germans had their orchestra, of course, but ours was forbidden. I'll tell you what. Why don't you come to my home this Saturday at five. You can play for me then." He gave me his address.

I could not wait for the days to pass. On Saturday I arrived a little early and had the pleasure of meeting Kubelik's wife while we waited for him to return home. She showed me his father's violin, a beautiful Stradivarius that hung from the ceiling in a glass enclosure. A composition student of Rafael Kubelik, Ilia Hurnik, was also there. We warmed up to each other so quickly that he gave me one of his compositions, which I still have. In such a beautiful home, among this charming company, I started to feel self-conscious about my ill-fitting refugee clothes, given to us by charity organizations. As I sat there waiting for Kubelik, I felt I looked like a clown. When we were liberated, all we had were our striped prisoner uniforms from the camp. So I ended up in somebody else's pants, somebody else's shoes, somebody else's shirt. Nothing really fit. They were all leftover clothes, already worn thin.

Kubelik arrived—a magnificent fellow, so tall he created a wind when he walked. He was all apologies for being late. "All right," he said to me. "Are you ready?" I sat down at the piano and played the Chopin E Minor Concerto from beginning to end. As I played, he never interrupted. From the corner of my eye, I could see him watching and listening to me intently. When I finished, he asked me, "Where is your music?"

"In Warsaw, burned up in my family's apartment with everything else—books, piano, clothes, everything. These clothes I'm wearing aren't really mine, Maestro. They were given to us at the refugee center. I don't have anything of my own."

"How long did you not play the piano?"

"Five years."

"But you did not make a single mistake!"

What could I say? I almost felt as if I should apologize. I had obviously impressed him both as a pianist and a personality because now he turned his attention to my personal welfare. "Let's forget about music for a minute," he said. "Where do you live? What do you do? How do you eat and survive?"

When I mentioned the name of the hotel where the city fathers had put us up, Kubelik burst out laughing. The hotel had been a notorious whorehouse used by the German soldiers. Well, whatever its previous use, it was a roof over our heads. However, the city was going to allow us to stay there for only a few more days. When I mentioned our dilemma to Kubelik, he made a quick phone call that fixed the situation by obtaining permission for my brother and me to stay at the hotel for as long as we wanted. Kubelik was a marvelous human being whom I loved immensely. I could not have dreamed then that six years later I would be performing with him in Chicago as he conducted the Chicago Symphony Orchestra.

With our housing situation now stable, thanks to him, I was free to concentrate my energies on practicing piano at the Conservatory. One lunchtime while I was waiting for Joel at a little restaurant where refugees liked to gather, I noticed a fellow who looked vaguely familiar. Could it possibly be my cousin from the Warsaw suburbs, the one whose father owned a bicycle factory? I hadn't seen him in, what, fifteen years?

"Excuse me," I said to him. "You look familiar. Is your name Joskowitz, by any chance?"

"Yes, it is."

"From Wyszkow?"

"Yes."

"Your family owned a bicycle factory?"

"That's right."

"Don't you recognize me?"

He stared at me as if he was working out the answer to a puzzle. Suddenly, he got it. "Marian, is that you?"

We fell into each other's arms. As we exchanged news, he mentioned that he had seen my brother.

"You've seen Joel? That's great. He'll be here any minute. We can all eat together."

"Joel is alive?"

"Of course he's alive. You just said you saw him. Who the hell are you talking about?"

"I'm talking about *Michael!* I saw him yesterday in Lodz. I just came from there this morning."

"Michael's alive?"

"Yes, he's alive. I talked to him."

I couldn't believe my ears. Michael had come back from a Soviet slave labor camp in Siberia!

When Joel arrived and I told him the news, it took us only a split second to decide what to do next. We went back to the hotel, packed our knapsacks, and went to the railroad yards to catch the next train to Poland. The borders were still open at this time, without checkpoints or guards.

We caught a night freight train that arrived in Lodz at six the next morning. Joel felt it was too much to carry the knapsacks around while we searched for Michael, so he pulled rank on me. "You sit here in the railroad station while I go look for him."

"Why you?" I said. "I want to go."

"You sit because you're the youngest and I'm the oldest. So I go and you sit." He could be such a dictator!

So while I waited at the station guarding our knapsacks, Joel went into town to look for the Jewish refugee center. He found it about an hour later, and although its doors were closed, the courtyard was open. Its walls were covered with hundreds of notes from refugees: "I've arrived. I'll be back at noon. N. P." and so on. Joel read each note until his eyes came to rest on familiar handwriting: "Michael Filar, Zawadzka 27, with Dr. Malamed."

A few minutes later Joel was knocking on the door of Zawadzka 27. This was the home of Jewish people who had survived the Nazis by escaping to the forests and fighting with the partisans, their grandmother with them the entire time. The grandmother answered Joel's knock.

"Does Mr. Filar live here?"

"Yes, but it's seven o'clock in the morning. He's still asleep. Why don't you come back later?"

"I'm sorry to disturb you, but he's my brother. I haven't seen him in five years."

"Oh, well then, come in."

Michael was sleeping on the sofa in the living room, with his left foot sticking out from under a blanket. So Joel tickled his foot. When Michael opened his eyes, he saw his oldest brother. You can't imagine how sorry I am that I wasn't there to witness their reunion.

Meanwhile, I was sitting in the railroad station fighting to stay awake after having been up all night. The knapsacks were on the floor next to me, while I kept nodding off. At one point a Russian soldier stuck his foot in the belt of one of the knapsacks and tried to pull it toward him without waking me up. I woke up just in time to see the knapsack moving away, so I shouted at the bum and he took off. From then on I made a point of keeping one eye open. About a half hour later, through that one eye, as if in a dream, I saw my two brothers coming toward me. I embraced Michael and cried with happiness. It was a miracle that all three of us survived and were together again.

Michael had an amazing story to tell. After the Russians sent him to a gulag in Siberia in 1940, he managed to survive until the Russian attitude began to change after the German invasion of the Soviet Union. With the Russians taking a beating and the Germans getting closer and closer to Moscow, the Russians knew they needed all the help they could get. They gave a Polish general named Anders permission to create an army from the former Polish military people in the gulags to fight against the Germans. Michael was lucky that he stayed alive long enough to join this Polish army. If Stalin hadn't agreed to Anders's idea, none of the Poles would ever have gotten out of Russia.

Michael and my sister Lucy and her husband Ben, who had been an army captain, left Russia with the Poles. In Tehran the three of them parted company with the Poles and went to Palestine, where they stayed with my brother George. When the war ended, Michael returned to Poland to search for what was left of our family.

Joel, Michael, and I stayed in Lodz with Dr. Malamed and his family for four weeks. During that time I took a train to Cracow to see Professor Drzewiecki, who was now director of the Conservatory of Music there, and to thank him for his help. It was a tearful, joyous reunion.

In those days you never knew when somebody you knew might turn up. Once when I was coming out of the Cracow Conservatory after seeing Professor Drzewiecki, I ran into a friend of mine from Cracow, Edward Bury, a composer who had studied in Warsaw. He looked at me, and his jaw dropped. "Filar! You mean they didn't kill you?" What a greeting! What was I going to say? Yes, they did, and I'm just a ghost? So I answered, "Edward, you mean they didn't kill *you?*"

The truth is that no one expected anyone else to survive, so when they did it was a miracle and a wonderful surprise. Dr. Lobaczewska survived, and I stayed with her for a couple of days in Cracow. But my old friend George Goldflam I'm sure did not survive because I would have known if he had. He would have contacted our teacher, and the fact that he never did makes me believe that they murdered him. After my visit to Cracow, I took the train back to Lodz.

Returning to Warsaw was out of the question since the city was almost totally destroyed and those who survived weren't there but were refugees in Lodz, Cracow, and other Polish cities. I wish I could say that as I was walking down the street one day, I saw my mother and my father and Helen and Ignaz, but I never did. In fact, I never had any hope that I would. In the ghetto we learned that once the Germans got you, that was it.

In mid-July 1945, about two months after my liberation, I played my first postwar concert with the Lodz Philharmonic Orchestra under the baton of Zdzislaw Gorzynski. I performed the Chopin E Minor Concerto, and it was a great success, but the public never realized how much I sweated over it—quite literally. For one thing, it was difficult for me to be inside public buildings. I remember how sweat poured off me in small rivers the first time I tried to sit still inside a movie house. And for the concert I had to perform in a big hall packed with people. When a doctor assured me that my problem would pass, I felt somewhat better. I was healthy enough, he explained, it was just that my two years in the camps had spooked me when it came to confinement. I'd get over it, he said, and I did.

Another problem had to do with the keys on the piano I was to play. They felt very heavy to my touch. When I mentioned this problem to a colleague, Jan Berezynski, he came up with the solution. "I know of a convent here in Lodz that has an old piano with keys so heavy you have to hit them with your feet. I'll arrange it so you can practice there. Then when you play the Philharmonic's piano, it'll seem easier." He turned out to be absolutely right.

After the concert I was surprised and delighted by a visit backstage from Dr. Eugene Morawski, the rector of the Warsaw Conservatory of Music, or I should say the former rector of the Conservatory, since the Germans had destroyed it and it had yet to be rebuilt. During lunch with Dr. Morawski the next day, he reminded me of a conversation we had had in his office seven years earlier, which seemed like a lifetime.

"Before the war, I told you that I believed in you. That you would have a great career. Do you remember?"

"Yes, I remember every word," I said.

"Now I'm going to tell you something else. Leave Poland. Go west, Marian. Listen to me! I believe you'll have a great career."

"Rector Morawski," I said, "I'll tell you a secret. I'm already packed. We're leaving tomorrow morning."

He kissed my head and said, "Be well."

The next day my two brothers and I left for Berlin, the first stop on our journey west.

A New Beginning in Germany

Before the war, I had never been to Berlin, even though it was a center of culture. From 1931 on, when the Nazis were becoming powerful, we stayed away from Germany. Now the once mighty Berlin was quite devastated. Whole neighborhoods were leveled, wiped out. Broken walls, broken buildings, broken streets, craters. The German bastion full of strutting Nazis was now swarming with Allied soldiers.

Soon after Joel, Michael, and I settled ourselves at a refugee center, I went off on my own to see the Reichstag, the German parliamentary building, which was now partly in ruins. On the ground in front lay the bust from the statue of one of the kaisers, with feces piled on it. On one of the still partially standing walls was a big sign in Russian, "Perfect work of the Soviet Air Force."

Standing on the partial ruins of the Reichstag, an old German

man was trying to explain the building's history to a group of about twenty high-ranking Allied officers—American, English, French, and Russian. I could tell by the expressions on their faces that nobody understood a word the old German was saying, so I offered to translate for the Russians and the French and apologized to the Americans and English for not knowing their language. But a French officer who spoke English was able to translate for them, so everyone was glad I was there.

Actually, the old German didn't know a lot about the Reichstag, but when he mentioned that near the Brandenburg Gate—only about a three-minute drive away—Hitler's *Reichskanzelei* (chancellery) was still intact, the officers became very interested in seeing it. When they insisted I come along as an interpreter, I was only too happy to oblige. On the way, the old German asked me if I was a Russian, and I said, "Sure. Straight from Moscow." I still wasn't ready to socialize with a German.

There was one burned-out armored car still in front of the Chancellery's front doors, and MPs from each of the four Allied countries stood guard. We had a number of high-ranking officers among us, so no one dared to stop our group from going in. We first went to the Nazi Party meeting hall, an immense room with an extremely long table running down its center with maybe eighty or a hundred chairs still set up along its sides. We then went to the end of the hall and entered Hitler's big private office.

Diagonally across from the entrance to the left was his desk and chair. A globe was on a little table to the right of the desk. In the film *The Great Dictator* there is a scene in which Charlie Chaplin, playing Hitler, contemplates a globe just like this one and uses it to dream about conquering the world. On the left was the entrance to Hitler's private washroom and a large black wall safe. The officers joked that the safe must hold all the diamonds and gold Hitler stole from across Europe. A very large and beautiful chandelier was hanging from the high ceiling.

When I sensed that one of the Russian officers might be Jewish, something in me wanted to let him know that I was Jewish too. I found a way of doing it by glancing at the chandelier and saying to him, "Sir, don't you think it would make a beautiful Chanukah lamp?" I could see in his eyes that he got it. It wasn't a big deal. I just felt I had found somebody, an officer and a Jew, whose family might have been murdered in Russia. Also in the room was a military bed that hung down from the wall on two chains, like a bed in a prisoner's cell. I don't know what it was for. Maybe Hitler used to nap on it.

As we were about to leave, a German caretaker in a green uniform came in from the garden and casually mentioned that the bunker where Hitler committed suicide was close by. We all wanted to see it, so we went out into the garden, turned right, and went about fifteen steps to the entrance. We descended about two floors into the concrete bunker in complete darkness, but since just about everyone was a smoker, we lit our way with lighters and matches. At the bottom the German in the green uniform pointed to a black door. "This is the room where he committed suicide."

We tried to open the door, but it was locked. One of the Russian officers said, "So what if it's locked? Let's break it down!" A half dozen big officers got ready to push in the door with their shoulders, and no one was going to keep me from joining in. So I squeezed in between them, and we started to push. One, two, three, boom! Nothing. It didn't budge. But that didn't stop us. One two three, boom! Three or four times. They were big strong guys, so we kept trying, and before you knew it, the door gave way. It was pitch-black inside. As my eyes adjusted, I made out a coffee table, some chairs, and a sofa. Figuring that Hitler had sat on the sofa, I went over and spit on it. How could I have ever dreamt when I was in Majdanek or Buchenwald that one day I would help break down the door to Hitler's bunker and spit on his sofa!

While we were in Berlin, we went to the movies and saw a newsreel I will never forget. Russian journalists were interviewing people on the street, asking, "Were you a Nazi?" "Nein, nein," they said.

He couldn't find a single one—hundreds of people and not one Nazi. Right after that, they showed captured newsreels with thousands of Germans yelling and cheering as Hitler rode down Berlin's main boulevard, everyone screaming and holding their arms out in that stupid salute. But ask them if they were Nazis, and no one knew what you were talking about.

Berlin was the first stop on our journey west. After staying there for a few days, Joel, Michael, and I moved on to Frankfurt and the American zone, which was our destination. There was such confusion and chaos in Germany at that time that we traveled the one hundred miles by bus through the Soviet zone to Frankfurt without once being questioned.

In Frankfurt I hoped to locate Alfred Hoehn, the great German pianist and teacher who had offered to take me to Germany to study with him when I was a kid. He was director of the Frankfurt Conservatory of Music, which was one of the reasons why we went to Frankfurt. My brothers and I were accepted at a displaced persons (DP) camp run by the United Nations Relief and Rehabilitation Administration in Zeilsheim outside of Frankfurt. They provided us with a small apartment with a big balcony and nice kitchen. Once I knew we had a roof over our heads, I went to the Conservatory to inquire about Mr. Hoehn, only to learn that he had died of a heart attack in the middle of a recital. So that was that.

I soon found consolation, however, when people at the DP camp brought me a piano, an old upright. It wasn't anything to write home about, but it had keys and was in tune, and now that I had a piano to practice on, I could dream of restarting my career. I would sit there in a little room, with a stovepipe protruding from the wall beside the piano, and repeat the Chopin E Minor Concerto over and over. Since this was only a few months after the liberation, I still didn't have any sheet music, and I could only play the compositions I had memorized.

This was a time of trial for me. For the first time in my life I was no longer certain if I should continue as a pianist. I was already twenty-seven years old. After all those years away from the piano, years without practice, could I still fulfill my early promise? I had always felt an attraction toward the ideals of the medical profession, and now I wondered which path I should follow. If I was to continue as a concert pianist, I needed to be sure I could meet my own highest standard. And it seemed to me I needed to be tested by someone who really knew what the highest standard was. I wanted to find such a person to hear me. I honestly didn't know if I still had it.

One day I went to a rehearsal of the Frankfurt State Radio Orchestra. Frankfurt State Radio was a large arts organization with its own orchestra and concert hall, and its conductor and members were all Germans certified by U.S. Army Intelligence as non-Nazis. As I sat listening to them play, it occurred to me that I had worked a damn long time for the Germans in their camps. Maybe one of them would now give me an audition or at least hear me play.

Although normally no one was allowed into a rehearsal, Americans and DPs could go anywhere in those days. No one dared stop us. Even when the orchestra performed publicly, only Americans, foreigners, and DPs were allowed to attend—no Germans. When the rehearsal ended, I approached the conductor, Hans Blümer, and told him a little about myself and asked if I might have an audition. He said okay, so after the other orchestra members left, I played the Chopin E Minor Concerto. I played for ten or fifteen minutes at most before he interrupted me: "That's enough. No need to play any more. You're hired." Not long afterward, I played the first of what would be quite a few concerts for the Frankfurt State Radio. As it turned out, a few months later Mr. Blümer was relieved of his post when it was learned he had lied about not having been a member of the Nazi Party.

While I was in the DP camp, I contacted the German who helped me survive, Mr. Ställer, who now lived in Welmerskirchen, near Cologne. He came and had lunch with me and my two brothers. With the war over, decent Germans like Mr. Ställer were having a hard time. He had helped me when I needed it, so I did my part to help him as I got better situated. I had food packages sent to his family from the United States and tried to help him out as best I could. It didn't surprise me to learn that before the war he had been an active Social Democrat and ardent anti-Nazi. Through the years I have remained in contact with Mr. Ställer's family.

I was asked many times later why I did not refuse to perform in Germany, as some Jewish artists such as Isaac Stern did. I shall let this book be my answer. Not all Germans were Nazis, not all Germans were bad. One of them saved my life—and my hands.

Later, when I contacted Mr. Ställer's daughter, I asked her if she had any information about the man who had been chief of the camp. I was still curious about him. Was he a Nazi or not? He probably was. He was a civilian and wore a swastika. Yet, after that time I played for him, he helped me. He certainly knew the backgrounds of the men in his camp, and yet he still sent me to Ställer, an anti-Nazi, which saved my hands. He couldn't have been a total rat. Unfortunately, there was nothing in Mr. Ställer's papers about the camp chief, so it will forever remain a mystery to me.

In Frankfurt I soon became friends with Heinz Schroeter, the director of the State Radio Chamber Music Department, and performed lots of solo work for him. I confided to him that I wasn't sure how to assess my talent after so many years without playing. Newspaper critics wrote wonderful reviews of my performances with the Radio Symphony Orchestra, but I wasn't sure who they were or how much they really knew. Just because someone is a critic doesn't always mean he knows that much about music. I told Mr. Schroeter that I needed to be tested by someone who was a truly great musician.

"Walter Gieseking, the greatest German pianist, lives in Wiesbaden," he said. "Forty minutes on the train, and you're there."

I knew he was right in his assessment of Gieseking's greatness. As a kid I had heard Gieseking play in Warsaw, and I never forgot it. "Do you know him?" I asked. "Could you give me a letter of introduction or something?"

"Oh, I know all about him, but he doesn't know anything about me. A letter from me won't do you any good. But I can find his address for you. I really think you should go see him."

I don't know if I would have spent so much time with Mr. Schroeter if I had known that he lied to me. I had once asked him what he did during the war. Of course, after the war everybody you talked to was only a simple soldier. Nobody was ever an officer or was involved in anything. "Oh, I wasn't in great physical shape," he said. "They drafted me six weeks before the end of the war." Years later in an interview in Philadelphia when he was visiting me, he said he had spent five years in the army. He had forgotten what he had told me, but I remembered. I didn't move a muscle or show anything. When I first asked him, it really had mattered to me. And he had lied.

Still, Mr. Schroeter did get me Gieseking's address and pushed me to go see him. But that was a lot easier said than done. When it came right down to it, I wasn't sure I had the guts. How did I know what Gieseking would be like? Maybe he was an anti-Semite and a Nazi. Maybe he would hate me. I knew he was a great pianist, but I didn't know anything else about him. And, being a great artist doesn't always mean that someone is a great person or even a very likable person. However, a German-Jewish lawyer in Frankfurt, Sid Gembicki, and his wife were able to help me with this matter. Mr. Gembicki was a wonderful man who survived the war in Canada and was now assistant provost marshal of Frankfurt as well as a great music lover. His wife, Louise "Lulu" Kahn Gembicki, had remained in Germany during the war despite being half-Jewish. The Nazis murdered her father, but her mother survived. Lulu also loved music very much, and we became close friends. One day I asked Lulu if she knew what Gieseking had done during the war. "You were here, Lulu. What was he doing? Was he a Nazi or something?"

"I never heard anything like that. However, I do recall going to hear one of his recitals, and, as a matter of fact, he played Mendelssohn's *Lieder ohne Worte*."

By Mendelssohn! Hearing that gave me courage. No anti-Semite would play the music of Mendelssohn, a Jew. So a few days later, I took a train to Wiesbaden to look for Gieseking. I was determined to find a way for him to listen to me play.

My first attempt to find 24 Wilhelminenstrasse, Gieseking's address, took me to a bombed-out area near the train station. What a strange neighborhood for a famous pianist to be living in, I thought. I found 2, 4, 6, 10 Wilhelminenstrasse, and then an empty field. "Oh, God, they gave me the wrong address," I thought. "I've come all this way for nothing." Fortunately, an old German lady passing by put down her shopping bag to help me.

"Don't worry," she said. "There's another Wilhelminenstrasse in Wiesbaden, a beautiful avenue just down the hill by the War Monument. You'll find it."

I did find 24 Wilhelminenstrasse all right, and it was indeed on a beautiful avenue. Entering through the gates of Gieseking's estate was like walking into a dream. He owned a gorgeous three-story villa set on five or six acres of land. Flower beds and blossoming cherry trees framed the walkway, and there was a large swimming pool shining in the sun.

I walked up to the main door, pressed the bell, and waited. Mr. Gieseking himself opened the door, all six feet, four inches of him. I looked up at him, took a breath, and began speaking German as fast as I could, afraid he might slam the door in my face. I told him I was a soloist with the Frankfurt State Radio Symphony and had received some beautiful write-ups. "May I talk with you?" I asked. "Could you offer me ten minutes of your precious time?"

Gieseking looked me up and down the way a man evaluates a horse before he decides to buy. "Come on in," he said. Well, I had made it over the first hurdle!

I followed him through the beautifully furnished entrance hall into his music room with its two magnificent grand pianos. He sat down behind his desk to get a better look at me and asked what I wanted.

"Professor, the first thing I want to tell you is that I am Jewish."
I thought, "If he doesn't like it, well, 'It's nice to know you,' and I'll
just walk out." He didn't react, so I went on. "Until recently, I
hadn't seen a piano for nearly five years. Now I'm back to practicing
and performing, but I'm just not sure what to do with myself. Five
years is a big hole in a pianist's life at my age. I'm also interested in
medicine. If you would be kind enough to listen to me play for just
ten or fifteen minutes, it would mean everything to me. If you tell
me I should quit, I'll go study medicine. And if you tell me to go
on, I'll go on—because to me you are the greatest pianist in the
world. I just need your opinion. It means my life to me."

"Oh, uh-huh, I see," he said. "You just show up unannounced,
knock on the door, and say you want to play. Do you think you're
the only one?" He opened his desk drawer, took out a thick pack of
letters, and put them on his desktop. "They *all* want to play for me.
But *they* write. From all over Europe they write. Why don't *you*
write?"

"Professor," I asked, "have you answered all those letters?"

That got a smile out of him. "It takes too much time to write to
everyone," he said.

I was encouraged by that little smile. "Yes, Professor, it's true I
took a chance coming to you without first writing. If you want me
to leave, I'll leave. I don't demand anything. I'm just asking for a
break."

"No! You should have written first. Don't you know they put me
on a blacklist? They said I was a Nazi. But it's a damn lie. A damn
lie! I had nothing to do with the Nazis!"

I couldn't believe my ears. He didn't know me from Adam, and
here he was getting angry at me because of something the Allies
had done to him.

"No, no," he went on, "you should have written!"

My spirits sank as I realized I was getting nowhere. What was I
to do? I was as poor as a church mouse, a stateless person without a
passport. The only other great German pianist I knew of was Wil-

helm Backhaus, who was living in Switzerland. Since I had no money for the train fare, Backhaus might just as well have been in China. And Backhaus wasn't as great as Gieseking. Besides, he had once been a confirmed Nazi, so that eliminated him. Before the war when Backhaus played in Warsaw, protesters picketed the concert hall because he was a Hitlerite.

Professor Drzewiecki told me an interesting story about this. Once the Gestapo came to his house in Warsaw, pushed their way in, and started looking around. On his wall they saw a framed photograph of Backhaus inscribed "To my dear friend Zbigniew Drzewiecki." The Gestapo looked at the photo and said, "Is Mr. Backhaus a friend of yours?" Professor Drzewiecki responded, "See for yourself." They saluted him and turned around and left.

As I rose to leave, I felt completely broken. If Mr. Gieseking wouldn't hear me, whom could I ask or turn to? With tears in my eyes that I could not suppress, I said to Mr. Gieseking, "Well, Professor, I didn't have any luck the last five years, and I'll probably not have any the rest of my life."

He saw the tears in my eyes, and that must have touched him. "Well, since you are already here," he said, "sit down and play something." Wow!

Mr. Gieseking opened one of his pianos for me, so I sat down and played Bach, then Mozart. Mr. Gieseking didn't comment. Then he said to me, "Since you're Polish, why don't you play some Chopin?"

I played the G Minor Ballade. Suddenly Mr. Gieseking was all smiles. He even put his arm around me. I'll tell you what he said next because I still remember exactly: "You want to give up the piano? You must be crazy. You are *already* a concert pianist. Would you like to study with me? Do you think I can teach you something?" Did he think he could teach me something? How could I *not* learn from him?

I almost cried. "Study with you? God, could I?" I had not dared let myself think of that possibility. "How much will you charge me for a lesson?" I had no idea where I'd get the money, but I was determined I'd find it one way or another.

Then he said the most amazing thing. "You've already paid enough. Come every Thursday at 10:30. You don't have to telephone because the phone doesn't work. Just ring the bell and come in."

So that was how I became Walter Gieseking's student, and he never took a cent from me. Later when I told Professor Drzewiecki that I was studying with Walter Gieseking, my old teacher congratulated me and said, "Marian, you've won the biggest number in the lottery!" And that's how I felt too.

A friend once asked me what I would have done if Mr. Gieseking had told me, "Go be a doctor." Would I have listened to him? Probably not, although I wouldn't have contradicted him. Music is my life. When I was in the camps, my music sustained me, although I never tried to practice in my imagination or massage my hands. Who had time or energy for that? You had to be a creative artist just to survive. You were fighting for your life twenty-four hours a day—not twelve, but twenty-four. You never knew when they would come in the middle of the night and kill you. They could do anything they wanted at any time, on any day of the week, at any minute of the day. I didn't even think about music. I lived for it, but I thought only about surviving minute to minute.

Walter Gieseking

On that first day, Gieseking invited me to lunch and I met his wife and two daughters, Freya and Jutta. I couldn't help but notice that now the shoe was on the other foot in Germany. It was the Germans' turn to eat very little. The Giesekings were eating nothing but potatoes, while we DPs, supplied by the American army, had food up to our ears.

This gave me an idea, so the next Thursday when I came for my first lesson, I brought a few cans of food with me from the DP camp. I figured that if he was going to teach me for free, the least I could do was show I was grateful. As I started to unpack the food, Gieseking looked at me sternly. "Why did you do that? You had nothing to eat for five years. It's you who needs food, it's you who needs to eat, it's you who needs strength to play the piano. You bring it once more, and you won't get a lesson."

"I'm sorry, Professor. I meant well."

"I know. It's all right."

But I had gotten the idea in my head to pay him in some way, and it wouldn't let go. So the next week I arrived fifteen minutes early for my lesson, and as I waited for Gieseking in the music room, I hid cans of food here and there, putting some behind books, some under a chair, some on the windowsill. I had my lesson and went home. The next week when I entered the music room for my lesson, he was looking at me with a little smile on his face. "You know," he said, "this has became a very funny room. I go to the window to see if it's raining, and I see on the windowsill a can of beef. Then I go to my bookshelf, and I find a can of butter." He was amused by the idea, but he wagged his finger at me anyway. "What did I tell you?"

"Professor, I'm embarrassed. It's just that I don't know how to thank you."

"Fine, fine. But don't bring any more. Really." Of course, I did not want to anger my teacher, so I didn't. He was a wonderful human being as well as a great artist. We hit it off right away.

Nonetheless, I have to admit that when I arrived for my first lesson with him, I was very nervous. To be honest, I was scared stiff. I knew I was studying with the greatest pianist in the world. I soon realized that he was more of a coach than a teacher, which was what I needed. He wasn't about to tell me, "This is a sharp, this is a flat," or explain to me the basics of music. If I hadn't already been a concert pianist, he wouldn't have bothered with me. He once told me, "If anybody ever says he studied with me before the war, tell him he's a liar."

Not long after one of my first lessons with Mr. Gieseking, I arrived at his home to find a Polish guard with a rifle standing on the grounds of the villa. Many Poles were working as guards for the U.S. Army at the time. When I asked him in Polish what was going on, he told me that the Americans wanted Gieseking to leave. Their plan was to take possession of the largest houses in that section of the city for their own use.

Inside I found Gieseking and his daughters packing the books and music they hoped to save from confiscation. "Professor," I said,

"I'm going to start a little diversionary action. I'll get a hold of the guard and tell him a few Polish jokes. He'll forget where he is." That's exactly what happened. While the guard was walking one way with me and laughing at my jokes, books and music were taken out the side doors. In a week or ten days the Americans changed their minds, so the order was rescinded and the guard was lifted.

When I grasped that Mr. Gieseking wasn't a teacher as much as a coach, I had my best idea. We would be working on a composition, and I would say something like, "Professor, would you be kind enough to play this page through?" And he always would. Boy, did I learn from that! Hearing him was the best lesson I could ever receive, an education in itself. Once when I stayed for dinner, he said to his wife, "When Filar comes, I end up playing a whole recital! A whole recital!" He kidded me about it, but he knew what I was doing.

So above all, I was learning by hearing Mr. Gieseking play. He had two beautiful grand pianos, both gorgeous instruments. The music that came out of them when Mr. Gieseking played was indescribable. It was as if he was perfuming the air with sound. He could reduce me to tears in a second with his playing.

I heard sounds I never heard on a piano before. Hearing Mr. Gieseking's pianissimo, a sound no one else makes, was unbelievable. He told me, "Learn the real pianissimo sound—go way down to the bottom of the key." He played it everywhere, but he especially played it in Schubert, Mozart, Ravel, and Debussy, or whatever else he played that required a really soft touch. He could go so far down that he reached the limit of sound. He played so softly you could barely hear it. In the concert hall people sat leaning far forward. "I think I hear it, but I'm not sure. Am I going crazy?" The amazing thing was that they *did* hear it. But it was just a hair above the level where you don't hear anything.

The beauty of it was that this pianissimo gave him a skill and dynamic range that were amazing. He was a big German man and very strong, yet he could play so very, very softly. Everybody can play the other end, the fortissimo end, and bang the hell out of the instrument. No one ever has any difficulty doing that, and for too many pianists that's all they do. But this pianissimo is something else—and the expressiveness of that softness is just exquisite.

And then there was his phrasing. He taught me the styles and phrasing of different composers, especially Brahms. What did I know about Brahms? I don't think I had ever played Brahms or Schubert in the Conservatory, or certainly not much. When I heard him play Brahms, I flipped. I thought, "My God, is that beautiful!" Brahms played like that can make you cry your eyes out. Studying with Mr. Gieseking opened up for me a whole new world of music and composers, and I heard them from the best source there is—a superb artist. I should add here that I learned how to play Brahms not only from Mr. Gieseking but also by accompanying the great singer, Aga Joesten, in Frankfurt. She taught me so much about the Brahms and Schubert lieder.

I learned my techniques from Professor Drzewiecki, but I learned my sound from Mr. Gieseking. For example, I didn't learn that much from Mr. Gieseking with respect to the style of playing Chopin, but I did learn a great deal about the tone quality of the sound. And this is the greatest thing you can have with Chopin because Chopin was able to make the piano sing like a human voice. I learned my singing tone from Mr. Gieseking. I didn't have it before. How could I have had it? I had never ever heard anything like it! And I had heard all the great pianists. I had heard *everybody*. I heard Hofmann, I heard Horowitz, I heard Rubinstein, I even heard Rachmaninoff. But Mr. Gieseking was a revelation with his unique tone quality.

And his Ravel and Debussy were out of this world. Mr. Gieseking was German, but he had been born in France and lived there till age seventeen and so had an affinity for French composers. Gieseking said of Debussy, "I am proud and happy that my name is often associated with Debussy's music, this marvelous music that seems to me so natural and perfect, so sincere and beautiful."

At the start of my studies with Mr. Gieseking, I wasn't sure what direction my lessons would take. I wanted to study the German composers—Bach, Mozart, Beethoven, Brahms, Schumann, Schubert. Then when I heard Mr. Gieseking play Ravel and Debussy, I was ready to quit and just say forget it. I sat there stunned. What a great artist Mr. Gieseking was. He played Ravel's *Gaspard de la Nuit* as if he had two hundred fingers. It's on a recording, but it's not the same as hearing it live, although it is better than nothing.

Gieseking once wrote about Ravel, "I feel boundless admiration and affection for the works of Maurice Ravel. Not only are they wondrously beautiful, but they contain the most pianistic music yet written and employ the resources of the modern piano in the most perfect and universal manner. Ravel will forever be among the great and glorious names of not only French but European music."

Hearing Mr. Gieseking play Ravel, I was in total despair. I told him, "Professor I'm going to shoot myself! I'm giving up and becoming a shoemaker! Who can hope to play like this? What am I doing here?" He laughed and said, "Yes, but I cannot play Chopin the way you do!" He was always so generous.

Mr. Gieseking suggested that I learn the Chopin F Minor Concerto. I knew the E Minor and had played it often, but not the F Minor. I also had Tchaikovsky and some Mozart concerti and a few other pieces in my repertoire. But Mr. Gieseking had said that I should know both Chopin concerti and also Beethoven's Third and Fifth (the Emperor Concerto). And what he suggested, I followed. So I went to work on the F Minor. I already knew the style and had an understanding of Chopin's music and an affinity with him. All I needed was a beautiful sound and that perfect tone quality, which I got from Mr. Gieseking. His tone quality was incomparable!

Once when I heard him play the Mozart C Major Concerto K.467 at a concert in Frankfurt, I was crying during the second movement. I couldn't hold the tears back. He was playing with just one hand with orchestra accompaniment. I sat there with tears streaming down my face, thinking "I'm dead and I'm in heaven. I don't know anything anymore. And I don't care." It was sublime.

One afternoon as I was sitting on the train returning from my lesson with Mr. Gieseking, going over in my mind what we had worked on, I realized that he was changing the way I played Mozart. Mozart was always one of my favorites. I had started with Mozart. And yet, when we worked together on the Mozart, Mr. Gieseking would point out things to me: "There's a phrase line here you overlooked, there's this and that." I thought, "He's changing my Mozart! Who the hell does he think he is? Professor Drzewiecki was the greatest teacher in Poland, and he never mentioned any of this." Mr. Gieseking never criticized: he was always extremely polite and just pointed out things—"You overlooked this, you didn't pay attention to that," just pointed out things very quietly.

I sat there on the train getting really annoyed at him. "Who does he think he is, changing *my* Mozart? I'm going to quit!" But then the other voice came into my head and said, "Just keep your mouth shut and listen. This is the greatest pianist in the world. You hardly touched a piano for five years. Maybe you forgot something, or maybe Professor Drzewiecki didn't teach you this. You don't know. Don't be stupid." I made up my mind that I'd better listen to Mr. Gieseking, and thank God I did.

After I had been studying with him for a while, he suggested I learn the *Barcarolle* by Chopin, which Mr. Gieseking had recorded. So I learned it as he asked, and he liked what he heard—very much so. He called in his wife, who was always the supreme judge. She was a few years older than he, and once she told me that when she started playing Debussy, Gieseking didn't yet know the composer's name. Before I started, he said loudly to her in my presence, "Filar studies with me and he plays the *Barcarolle* better than I do." After I finished playing it for her, she said, "Yes, that's right," and turned and walked out. I was very embarrassed. I said, "Professor, please don't say such things." I couldn't believe I could do anything better than Mr. Gieseking.

But that incident was so typical of him. He was always generous with his compliments and very kind and pleased for me. One time I played a recital for the American Red Cross in Frankfurt, and two or three weeks later Mr. Gieseking played a recital for them as well. Because of a misunderstanding over transportation, Mr. Gembicki and his wife and I arrived late. It was spring and very warm. All the windows of the building were open, and hundreds of people were standing outside the windows, five and ten people deep, to hear Walter Gieseking play.

We slipped in the side door, and a woman from the Red Cross recognized us. "It's packed," she said, "but I'll tell you what I'll do. I'll put three chairs in front of the first row and you can sit there." When the first piece was over and everybody was clapping, they set the chairs up and we tiptoed in and sat down. Lieutenant General Clarence R. Huebner was sitting in the first row with his wife and daughter. At the time I didn't know he was commander of the American forces in Europe, but I knew he must be very important when I saw all the stars and ribbons on his uniform.

When Mr. Gieseking saw us sit down, he stood up and announced, "Now you're going to hear played the Chopin A-flat Ballade," and gestured to me, saying, "Come up here and play it for me."

I turned bright red—like a tomato. "Professor," I said, "please don't. I'm going to jump out the window. Please."

Still, he insisted, "No, no, come up here and play it for me."

I wanted to crawl under my chair. "I won't do it. Please don't ask me." Of course, I wouldn't do it! But how incredible of him to make the offer in the middle of his own recital and single me out in front of so many influential people. But that was Mr. Gieseking. He was a wonderful person as well as a great artist.

In a number of ways he was one of the most amazing men I ever met. He had an incredible photographic memory. He knew more music than most people can possibly imagine or dream of—volumes worth. And yet he never practiced. Once he was scheduled to perform the Brahms Second Piano Concerto, the most difficult thing in the world, in Paris with the Orchestre Colonne under Gaston Paulet's baton. He was to play it on a Sunday. I saw him every day of the preceding week and had lunch and dinner with him and his wife at the Hotel George V, and I never saw him practice once! He didn't play, he didn't have a piano in his room, he couldn't care less. By Friday I was getting a little nervous, so I said to him, "Professor, you're not playing a little Haydn concerto, you're playing a known bone-breaker, the Second Brahms. You haven't touched the piano for a whole week. I'm getting scared." He laughed and said, "Who practices?" Rubinstein used to say, "If I miss practicing one day, I know it. If I miss two days, my conductor knows it. If I miss three days, my *audience* knows it!" But Gieseking didn't believe that. He never practiced before a rehearsal. That was just his way.

So, Gieseking went to his first rehearsal with the Orchestre Colonne without having touched the piano for a week. When we arrived, another rehearsal with the Polish pianist Jan Smeterlin was already in progress in the hall. Smeterlin was rehearsing Beethoven's Fourth Piano Concerto in G Major, a concerto for which Mr. Gieseking had just received a gold record. We walked in as Smeterlin was finishing the third movement, and right away I heard that his playing was anything but great—that's all I'll say. I thought, "Well, if I'm not crazy about it, Mr. Gieseking must really be suffering." When I sighed barely audibly, just a slight exhale, right away Mr. Gieseking leaned over to me and said very quietly, "When you have nothing good to say about a colleague, don't say anything at all."

When Smeterlin finished, he walked down the stage stairs on the far side and left, and Mr. Gieseking walked up the other stairs and sat down at the same piano, ready to play the Brahms Second Piano Concerto—no warm-up, nothing. After the orchestral introduction Mr. Gieseking started to play, and I almost fell out of my chair. He sounded as if he had been playing that concerto ten hours a day for the past week!

And the piano! It was the same piano Smeterlin had just played. I couldn't believe it! I leaned over to André Puglia, Mr. Gieseking's manager, and said, "Is this the same piano? If I hadn't been here to witness this with my own eyes, I wouldn't think it possible! That piano was dead. Now it sounds so alive, I can't believe it." The transformation was a miracle. I sat there flabbergasted. I was at a total loss for words. Mr. Gieseking had the ability to do that to me—and I'm not often left without words.

The same thing happened when I saw Mr. Gieseking sight-read. He was known as an incredible sight-reader, phenomenal, but my first experience of seeing him demonstrate this skill left me totally speechless. I was in the middle of a lesson when Mr. Gieseking told me that a young composer from Hamburg was stopping by. "He composed some sonata and he begged me just to read it and give him an opinion, and I couldn't refuse. He'll be here any minute. Do you mind?" That's how nice and polite Mr. Gieseking always was.

So this young fellow, a little older than I, came in and put his music on the stand. I was standing back from the piano a little bit, but I could see that the manuscript was handwritten and hard to read. "What the hell is that," I wondered? "Is it supposed to be music?" I couldn't make out the difference between a note and a rest, or whether something was a half note or a quarter note or what it was. Was someone supposed to play this? I couldn't figure it out at all. Mr. Gieseking sat down, and he didn't just *read* it, he *played* it—as if he had known it for ten years. I thought, "I don't believe this. Who's trying to kid me? It isn't human. This can't be real. He's playing a joke on me." I actually got mad, and when the composer left, I stuttered and finally blurted out, "Professor, you mean you never saw that music before?"

"No, I never saw it before. He just finished it a couple of days ago."

There was a pause, a long pause, and I looked at him and said, "Well, that's very nice, do you have any shoes to be fixed?"

"What do you mean?"

"What do I mean? I'm becoming a shoemaker, that's what I mean. Who can compete with this? I looked at the same music you did, and I couldn't tell if those were notes or rests or quarters or halves or if Picasso had painted it. And you played it like you had known it ten years! I don't get it. I give up. I'm in the wrong profession!"

He laughed and gave me his favorite answer, "Yes, but I can't play Chopin the way you do." That was always his answer when I felt frustrated. Mr. Gieseking loved it when I kidded him like that. He just loved it, he really did. And the madder I got, the more he laughed. He had a great sense of humor.

Once when he was recording a new piece for radio, he had a few people on the stage with him, including his daughters and myself. After he finished, he called the maintenance man over and asked for a long broom. The poor guy was flabbergasted. "A broom? It's not clean here, Maestro?" "I didn't say that. Just bring me a broom." The orderly disappeared and returned with a broom, which he nervously handed to Mr. Gieseking. Gieseking reached the broom under the piano and began sweeping. Then he looked over at us and said, "I'm cleaning up all those wrong notes that fell under the piano during the last movement." He burst out laughing, and so did the rest of us. He hadn't played one single note wrong! Those were fun times.

Enter Sol Hurok

During my first years in Frankfurt I practiced in a small room of our apartment, first on an upright piano and then on a five foot, seven inch Shiedmayer grand piano that Mr. Gembicki lent me. The Shiedmayer was not a bad piano, but it wasn't great. However, things changed in 1948 when I acquired one of the finest old grand pianos in the world—a Steinway C, a salon grand, which at seven feet, five inches is six inches longer than today's standard, the Steinway B.

I had begun thinking I ought to purchase my own piano after a conversation with Mr. Carmel Offie, a State Department political adviser to the American authorities in Germany. He was also the right-hand man of William C. Bullitt, the first U.S. ambassador to the Soviet Union during the Roosevelt administration. Judge Louis E. Leventhal, a Philadelphia judge who had the post in Frankfurt as the American government's political adviser on Jewish affairs, had introduced me to Mr. Offie. One day he asked me to do him a favor. Since he would soon be going back to the States, where pianos were much more expensive than in Germany, would I be willing to put an ad in the papers and see if I could find a good piano for him? He'd pay for it, of course, and then have the piano shipped back to Washington. I said I'd be only too happy to help.

Unfortunately, I couldn't locate anything decent before it came time for him to return to the United States. But I began thinking that if Mr. Offie found pianos expensive in America, how would I be able to afford a piano when I went there? By that time, my brothers and I had pretty much decided we would go to America sooner or later. So I put ads in the newspapers to find a piano for myself.

One of the first responses I got was an older woman who telephoned to say she had a piano I might be interested in, but it was outside the city at her son's house. When I went there, I saw the name Hoehn on the door. "Pardon me," I said to the man who answered the door, "are you by chance the son of Professor Alfred Hoehn?"

"Yes, I am."

"Alfred Hoehn, the great pianist and teacher?"

"That's right."

"Years ago, when your father returned from Warsaw, do you remember him telling you about a little boy who might be coming to live with you and study piano?"

"Yes, I vaguely recall something about that."

"Well, I am that little boy."

He showed me the piano, but unfortunately it wasn't very good, so I had to refuse it. It would have been wonderful to have inherited Alfred Hoehn's piano, but it was not to be. In fact, for the most part the pianos I was seeing were junk.

Then I received an intriguing message from a doctor. "I have a beautiful Steinway grand, seven feet, five inches long, model C. If you want a *good* piano, this is it." So I went to the doctor's elegant apartment near the main railroad station in Frankfurt am Main. The maid answered the door and asked me to wait in the salon.

"The doctor will see you in a minute," she said. "He's getting dressed." I went into the salon and feasted my eyes on a beautiful Steinway, maybe eighty years old, with the round piano legs of that period. When I opened it up and looked at the hammers, I could see that the felts did not have a scratch on them. The piano had hardly been used! The moment I began to play it, I knew I had found a great instrument.

As I was playing, the doctor entered the salon. "Mr. Filar, I'm asking a lot for it, but you'll pay every penny."

"How do you know my name?" I asked.

"I've heard you many times on the radio and in concert."

"I see. And how much do you want for the piano?"

"Six thousand new marks." This was 1948, and six thousand new marks wasn't chicken feed. The old mark, with Hitler's picture on it, which we were now using as toilet paper, had been changed to the more valuable new deutsche mark. The banks were trading one new mark for forty old marks.

"Where am I going to get six thousand marks?"

"If you want this piano, and I'm sure you do, you'll find the money."

"How about giving me a break on the price?"

"No. You'll pay every penny. You won't find another piano like it." A shrewd guy and a tough bargainer.

Like many people in Germany after the war, I knew a fellow who was a black marketer, so I went to him for help. I found him on the street carrying a violin case. "*You* play the violin?" I asked.

"Who plays the violin? I've got money in there, but the cops think I'm a violinist."

"Look, I need your help," I told him. "I'm buying a piano, and the man wants six thousand new marks. Is there anything you can do?"

"I tell you what, I know what a fine pianist you are, so I'll help you out. Give me four hundred American dollars. I won't make a cent on you. I just want to help you." I had some savings accumulated from concert fees, so I scraped together the money and got it to him. In return, he brought me a suitcase full of money—six thousand marks in tens and twenties. So I brought it to the doctor's house and purchased my piano, which was so large that I had to rent a room for it in a German neighbor's house.

In October 1948 I made my first visit to Paris. What can I possibly say about Paris? C'est jolie. C'est absolument fantastique. It's one of my favorite cities and one of the most beautiful in the world. And since the Germans occupied it for most of the war, it didn't suffer the destruction so many other European cities did.

The night train from Frankfurt arrived at the Gare de l'Est, one of the major train stations of Paris, at around seven in the morning. Arriving with twenty dollars to my name and no addresses or telephone numbers, just hope, my plan was to search for my cousins, who I knew lived there somewhere. Using my high school French, I left my luggage at the station and did what every visitor to Paris should do. I had breakfast at a small bistro with a cup of coffee and a newspaper and then went out for a stroll and a bit of sight-seeing.

I walked down the magnificent Champs Élysées, which had little traffic. Shimmering in the early morning light, the city was all I had imagined it to be. Then all of a sudden as I was walking, I felt someone touch me on my shoulder.

"Marian?"

I turned and saw a former boyfriend of my sister Helen. Out of the blue, just like that.

"What are you doing in Paris?" he asked me.

"I came to find my cousins. Do you know them?"

Not only did he know them, he had their phone number. What luck! Only a few hours after arriving in Paris, I had found my cousins and had a place to stay!

One cousin, Rymer, was a doctor and chief of a hospital, and he knew some people in the music world. They arranged for me to get a key to one of the three small downstairs halls sometimes used for recitals and rehearsals in the Salle Pleyel, which is to Paris what

Carnegie Hall is to New York. Suddenly I had use of a very good piano on which to practice.

These same people found out that a big classical music manager was coming to Paris from New York to scout for talent in Europe—an impresario of some kind. His name was Sol Hurok, which didn't mean anything to me. In fact, I wasn't up to date at all on what was happening in America. But through the American Jewish Joint Distribution Committee, which was operating in Paris at the time, an appointment was somehow arranged for me with this American manager for ten o'clock on a Friday morning.

I must say, Hurok didn't make a very good first impression on me. He came across as arrogant, pushy, and rude. The best thing about him was that he didn't spit when he yelled. Since I didn't know any English and he was of Russian origin, we spoke to each other in Russian, with a little German on the side. The American who introduced me to Hurok started off by saying, "Mr. Filar is studying in Wiesbaden with the greatest pianist in the world, Walter Gieseking."

Hurok nearly jumped out of his skin. He shouted, "You're studying with that Nazi?"

I suddenly felt on the defensive. "I don't know that he's a Nazi," I said. "I've inquired. A Jewish lady told me she heard him play Mendelssohn's *Lieder ohne Worte*. His manager was a Jewish fellow, a Mr. Bernstein. In fact, Gieseking paid him his commission during the war, even when Bernstein wasn't allowed to work for the pianist. That doesn't sound like a Nazi to me. And I understand Gieseking was cleared by U.S. Army Intelligence. As a matter of fact, he just received a visa at the American Embassy here. He's playing a recital at Carnegie Hall next January."

Hurok wagged his index finger at me vigorously. "He's *not* playing in Carnegie Hall. *I'm* telling you that." Boy, had I started out on the wrong foot! Still, he wanted to hear me play, so a time was set for an audition on the following Monday at my practice room in the Salle Pleyel.

On the day of the audition I arrived early, only to find that the piano I had been practicing on had been changed, a very fine instrument replaced with a very average one. When I asked what had happened, they told me that the Mozart Concerto for Two Pianos had been performed in the main concert hall the previous evening, so the management had taken my piano upstairs to the big hall. "But don't worry," they told me. "We'll have it back for you tonight."

"Tonight is too late," I said.

Hurok arrived with a retinue of photographers and musicians he was looking to take to America. He was in the middle of a big European talent hunt. I told him what happened, but he wanted to hear me anyway. So I played some Mozart and some Chopin for him, and I believe he liked my playing quite a lot. He certainly acted as if he did and had his photo taken with me—the only performer he had himself photographed with that morning.

"I'd like to take you to the States," he said. "Are you willing to be hungry for the first five years?" I got angry when I heard him say that. I still had no idea who or what Sol Hurok was. All that was apparent to me was that this rich uncle from America was offering me hunger all over again. I held my tongue and didn't answer his question.

"Mr. Hurok," I said, "I want to perform more for you first, so you'll know what my playing is like. If you've liked me on this piano, I'm sure you'll like me even better on my own piano in Frankfurt, a beautiful eighty-year-old Steinway C, a gorgeous instrument. Will you be coming to Frankfurt, by any chance?"

"As a matter of fact, I'll be there next week," he said. "Give me your phone number. I'll call you when I arrive." So I did.

Now it happened that Gieseking was also in Paris at that time to get his U.S. visa for his American recital. At dinner at the Hotel George V that evening with him and his wife, I mentioned that I had met Sol Hurok.

"You've met my number one enemy," he said. I hadn't known

anything about it. I described to Gieseking how Hurok had waved his arms around excitedly, vowing that Gieseking, would not play in Carnegie Hall.

"Maybe you shouldn't go to America yet," I suggested. "Maybe it's too early?"

"No, I'm going. If I don't go, they will *really* think I have something on my conscience, but I don't." The subject was dropped.

Gieseking invited me to attend a party the following Sunday at the apartment of a Parisian music critic, M. Belliard, and his friend, Mme. Milleret, who was a professor at the Paris Conservatory and a famous voice teacher. Their home was a center of music in Paris. "You will meet a lot of important people in the Paris music world," Gieseking told me. Of course, he was right. I played piano at the party and made friends. When I told M. Belliard that Hurok had offered to take me to America if I was prepared to be hungry for five years, he got red in the face. "He said that to *you?* He asked you to go there to be hungry? After all you've been through? You should have slapped him! You don't need Hurok to take you to America. You live in the American zone, so you'll go there anyway. Haven't you heard that President Truman has passed a law that those who survived the camps will be allowed to come to the United States? You need Hurok like a hole in the head. Forget him. Anyway, don't go back to Frankfurt yet. We have an audition set for you with the Orchestre Colonne, one of the best symphonies in Paris."

I thought to myself, "Maybe he's right. He's older and has a lot more experience in these matters than I." So I stayed in Paris, auditioned for Gaston Paulet, was engaged, and performed as soloist with the Orchestre Colonne. I played the Chopin F Minor Concerto on January 15, 1950. It was a grand success, with wonderful notices in the Paris press.

When I returned home to Frankfurt, my brother Michael said that Sol Hurok had telephoned for me while I was away. "I told him you were still in Paris, and he hung up." As subsequent events proved, I apparently made an enemy by not being there to receive his call. And I *still* didn't know who this Sol Hurok was supposed to be.

While I was back in Frankfurt, Gieseking was in New York, where he stayed at the Sheraton in preparation for his scheduled concerts. Across the street at Carnegie Hall, demonstrators marched with signs protesting his appearance. Their posters had "Nazi!" written under Gieseking's name, while Carnegie Hall's posters had "Sold Out" written across them.

At around seven in the evening, as he was getting into his tails in preparation for his first scheduled recital, there was a knock on his door. Immigration authorities came in and asked to see his visa. "Mr. Gieseking," they told him, "there's something wrong with your visa. You have to come with us to Ellis Island."

"There's nothing wrong with my visa. It was issued at the American Embassy in Paris. I know what's going on. I'm not a child. I know all about the protest in front of Carnegie Hall. Do I have a choice in this? Because I don't want to be taken to Ellis Island."

"We can't stop you if you want to go back to Europe."

So Gieseking never did play on his first postwar visit to the United States. The next morning he took a cab to the airport, got on an Air France plane, said "Vive la France!" and left. The press ran after him through the airport like yelping little puppies: "Mr. Gieseking, aren't you sorry you won't be able to earn a lot of money in America?" He said, "I make plenty of money all over the world. No problem." Mr. Gieseking returned to the United States in 1953 and performed to standing-room-only audiences without any problems.

I was driving in Frankfurt in the little Opel car I had bought when I heard a newspaper boy call out, "Gieseking arrested in America! Ten pfennig!" When the day for my lesson arrived, I telephoned Mr. Gieseking with not a little trepidation. "Well, Professor," I said, "You probably don't want to see me anymore. The Jews had you kicked out of the States, and that's it for me, right?"

"Marian, don't be silly. Come and see me right now."

"Okay, Professor, I'm on my way."

About ten minutes after I arrived at his villa, about twenty German reporters showed up, their pads and pencils at the ready. I was caught up in an interesting scene with Gieseking and the reporters. "Mr. Gieseking," they began, "tell us what happened in America."

"I will tell you nothing," he said. "I'm sick and tired of having interviews where the press puts words in my mouth, and then I'm accused of things I didn't say. I will tell you what happened under one condition only—I write it. And you don't delete or change one word."

I smiled, and then all of a sudden the German press people began to focus on me. "Who's this?" one asked. Gieseking could have used me beautifully: "Oh, he's a Jewish fellow who survived Buchenwald, and he's my favorite student," or some such thing. And I *was* his favorite student. Instead, he just said simply that I was one of his students and was there to have my lesson. German newspapers did end up giving him the opportunity and space in their pages to explain in his own words what had happened in New York.

This was one of only two times I ever saw Walter Gieseking particularly bothered by his enemies or critics. In this he was quite different from Arthur Rubinstein, who allowed critics' remarks to cut him far beyond what one would expect. Mr. Gieseking was almost always calm and philosophical, good-natured, and polite. But when he said something, he said it precisely right. Underneath his amiable manner, however, he had a fierce temper, which I saw explode in Manhattan during his visit in 1956. In December 1955 he had been traveling with his wife on a bus in Germany when fog caused the bus to slam into a highway pillar. His wife was sitting next to the window and was killed instantly, and Mr. Gieseking sustained cuts on his head from the broken glass. When I walked into his hotel room when he came to New York, his face was bright red. He was angry after having just finished reading a newspaper critic who ridiculed the way he looked, performing with a Band-Aid on his head. He was lucky even to be alive and able to play! Sometimes critics don't seem to have *any* intelligence.

The furor over Gieseking's first postwar visit to America indirectly provided me with still another confirmation that my teacher had had no avoidable dealings with the Nazi Party. Gieseking took care of the widow of his own teacher, Karl Leimer. She lived in his house and taught piano to a few students, one of whom, Maria Feltsmann, became a good friend of mine. Maria's older sister, a strikingly beautiful woman, was a budding movie star. Her boyfriend was a Jewish-American army major, Dubensky, who was in charge of music and arts in occupied Germany after the war. He checked out and passed on all the books, films, radio programs, and so on. When the flap over Gieseking occurred in New York, Major Dubensky became curious about the pianist and flew to army headquarters in Berlin, where they had the complete Nazi Party membership files, and searched them thoroughly. No Walter Gieseking. His name was subsequently completely cleared.

Farewell to Europe

The only problem with my studying with Professor Gieseking was that it was keeping my brothers and myself from taking advantage of American laws allowing concentration camp survivors to emigrate. We knew the window of opportunity could close for us if we acted as if we didn't want to go. Luckily, God provides. One day I received a telephone call from an American who said he'd like to study piano with me. He had been working for the U.S. government in Paris before being transferred to Frankfurt. He said Parisians who knew my playing had recommended me.

"Why don't you come on over?" I said. "We can talk about it more."

He stopped by, and since he seemed like a really nice fellow, I agreed to take him on as a student. "By the way," I asked him, "what kind of work do you do here?"

"Oh, I'm the new consul in the American zone in charge of emigration to the United States."

I nearly fell out of my chair! "God sent you! I'll be *glad* to teach you, and you don't have to pay me anything. You see, I'm studying with a fantastic pianist, Walter Gieseking, and I don't want to cut this opportunity short. My brothers and I want to emigrate to America all right, but not just yet. Can you hold our papers back?"

"No problem."

Joel wanted us to go, and the sooner the better, but Michael emphatically argued that we should stay in Germany. "You're making a great career in Germany," he told me. "You're nearly worshiped here as an artist." The Germans were different now that the Hitler hysteria was gone. They had always been tremendous music lovers, and since the war ended, the situation had changed. "Everything is different now," Michael said, "and you should take advantage of it. Why rush off? You have concerts, you already have a car and a piano, plus you are being invited everywhere." And it was true. It was a wonderful life. It really was. At that time Mr. Gembicki had parties almost every week.

Besides being the assistant provost marshal of Frankfurt under the Americans, Mr. Gembicki was an ardent music lover and, conveniently, a multimillionaire. He bought a villa, put a beautiful Steinway in it, and turned his house into a music center, a salon filled with marvelous wine, food, and song. Opera singers, American generals, and symphony musicians all went to his wonderful parties. The commander of the American army in Europe, Lieutenant General Clarence Huebner, also went there. He was a great friend of Mr. Gieseking. Judge Leventhal, the U.S. government's adviser for Jewish affairs in Germany, also attended. Everyone always had a wonderful time.

I told Mr. Gieseking about these evenings. There was great food—which nobody had back then—and all the wine and drinks you wanted. Mr. Gieseking liked to have a little drink now and again, so after he finally agreed, I took him there. The appearance of Walter Gieseking at the party caused quite a stir. When he walked in, jaws dropped. Two divas from the opera were immediately beside themselves. "Oh, Mr. Gieseking, if we had known you were coming, we would have brought our music with us."

"Don't worry about it, ladies," he said. "What would you like to sing? Let's go." He sat down at the piano and played the introduction from any opera they wanted and every aria they requested, accompanying their singing as if they had all been creating music together for twenty years! And what an accompanist! Any singer should have such an accompanist for five minutes! After it was all over they fell on their knees—I saw it with my own eyes—and kissed his hands and wept. Mr. Gieseking created this sort of atmosphere among singers and musicians. In their world, he was God.

Few people in America have any idea what it meant in Europe to be a classical musician. One warm spring day in Frankfurt I had my apartment windows open as I was playing the piano when suddenly I thought that I'd better close them so I didn't disturb anybody. I had hardly finished closing them when the phone rang: "Mr. Filar, we are your neighbors from across the street. Why did you close your windows? Please keep them open as much as you like—we love to hear you play."

This was the way things were. And, because things seemed to be working out for me, Michael wanted us to stay in Germany. Michael was everything to me. He was my father, my mother, my sister, my brother, my uncle—you name it. He had some money when he found us in Lodz, and that's when it started being a little easier for me. Joel had been bugging me to get a job, but Michael told him, "Get off his back! He's a pianist. He's going back to music. I have the money to pay for things, and the rest is none of your business. Let him alone!"

But as comfortable as things were, Joel and I didn't particularly want to stay in Germany. We still had bad feelings and bad memories. Michael had been in Siberia, so he didn't feel the same way. He tried to persuade us to stay, but Joel always said no. And Joel was the boss. Always. He was the oldest. What he said, went. As long as my piano student consul remained in Frankfurt, however, our papers were held back, and I was able to continue studying with Mr. Gieseking and not worry about going to America just yet.

Mr. Gieseking considered me his best student and helped advance my career in many ways. He wrote wonderful letters of introduction and recommendation, such as the one he wrote for me the very first year:

I declare herewith that Mr. Marian Filar, who has studied with me now for about a year, is an exceptionally gifted young pianist whom I expect with certainty to have a brilliant career as a soloist. Marian Filar has not only attained unusually high technical perfection in his piano playing, his musicianship aids him to find deep and complete understanding of the finest artistic qualities of the compositions he performs. His interpretations of Chopin's works are already among the finest I have ever heard. I expect him, if his talent is given the full possibility of development, to become a pianist of the first rank, and I hope and wish that every help will be given everywhere to such a promising young artist.

Walter Gieseking
Wiesbaden
January 25, 1947

He believed in me so much that he arranged concerts for me. Once when he returned from performances in Portugal, he announced that he had arranged concerts for me at Lisbon's Opera House and in three other cities during the 1949 commemoration of the one hundredth anniversary of Chopin's death. "They asked me if I knew somebody who played Chopin well. Since Arthur Rubinstein can't be everywhere at once, you're going!" So I went.

One of the first things I did after I arrived in Lisbon was to visit the Opera House to examine the piano I was expected to play. I was amazed and disappointed to find a very old Steinway without much sound, not a piano fit for a recital. So I told my manager, Mr. Quesada, that I wasn't satisfied with the piano and asked him if he could replace it.

"You don't like this piano? *This* piano?"

"No, it's too old."

"Well, take a look inside it."

"Why should I look? I can *hear* it."

"No, no, please, look inside. I want you to look."

So I looked inside. On the sounding board were signatures of the great pianists who had played it. Paderewski was there, Joseph Hofmann, Wilhelm Backhaus, Arthur Rubinstein. I stared and looked and examined and kept staring and looking and examining.

"Well," Mr. Quesada said, "haven't you seen them all yet?"

"No, I haven't. I'm still looking for one more name."

"Who are you looking for?"

"I'm looking for the signature of Johann Sebastian Bach—that's how old this damn piano is!" He almost fell on the floor, laughing. For that joke I got to perform on a new Steinway.

My performances were great successes and got me front-page reviews. After Lisbon I played in Oporto and at universities in the cities of Quimbra and Santarem. Since I arrived in Oporto a day early, the manager said, "Would you like to see a Catholic cathedral built in stone in the tenth century?" I said, "Sure, I love architecture." A little earlier, when we had passed an old synagogue, he had said, "You see this? There are no Jews here. I wonder why they don't tear that old building down." So I already knew what I was dealing with.

It was about ten o'clock in the morning when we entered the beautiful cathedral. Inside I thought to myself, "Now he's going to kneel, and I'm going to have a problem." When he genuflected and went into a pew, I went into the pew right behind him because I didn't want to embarrass him by not kneeling. When he knelt down, I remained standing behind him, so the problem was avoided because he didn't know if I was kneeling or not.

My emerging reputation as an outstanding interpreter of Chopin's music brought me more commemorative concerts. That same year I was chosen from all the pianists of Europe to be the soloist at Germany's gala one hundredth anniversary commemorative concert of Chopin's death. The concert, with Hermann Abendroth conducting the State Opera Orchestra, took place at the Opera House in Berlin on October 17, 1949, one hundred years to the day after Chopin died. All four ambassadors from the occupying powers attended the concert, and it was broadcast throughout Europe.

When I had first learned that Abendroth would conduct, I was scared stiff. He and Furtwängler were the two greatest conductors in Europe. You might expect that our first meeting would have been difficult. Abendroth was a German, and I was Polish and a Jew. He was an East Berliner, and I was staying in West Berlin—there was no wall yet. But when I met him, it was as if I had found an old grandpa. He was so considerate and kind, a wonderful man who asked *me* how I'd like to be accompanied. What a turn of events. Just a few years earlier I had been beaten and close to death in the camps of Nazi Germany, and now here I was, a Jew playing in Berlin!

In late 1949, after I returned to Frankfurt from my performances in Portugal, I learned that my student, the American consul in charge of emigration, had been transferred to another post. Not long afterward my brothers and I received letters telling us to come see the new consul. My brothers elected me to go and represent the three of us.

The new consul, a Jewish fellow, was angry at me. "How come the three of you are still here?" he demanded. "It's been more than three years! Boats are coming into New York half empty, and Congress is complaining about it. If you Filar brothers don't take the next boat, I promise you, you'll never get to the United States."

With that information I went back and told Joel and Michael, "Gentlemen, let's start packing." That was January 1950. One month later we were on the U.S. military transport ship *General Greeley* on our way to America.

Had I considered going to anyplace other than America? Yes. I had a married brother and a married sister in Israel. We had lost everything except each other, so where would I really want to be first? With my family. I had written to my sister Lucy and said, "We don't know what to do or really where we should go. I don't know anybody in America. I don't speak English. What do you think?" She wrote back, "As much as I love you and would like to see you, there is no future for you here in Israel. This is a country that is just starting. We are building roads and houses in Israel today. We need architects, we need engineers. Who's interested in music now? You'll be lost here. Go to America—as much as it hurts me to say it. We'll see each other later, but there is no future here for you now. Nothing."

George said pretty much the same thing. "What are you going to do here?" he wrote. "Work on the roads? Put stones in the street? We're telling you, in Israel no one has time for classical music. Maybe later on, when the country develops, but not now. Go to America."

So we decided it was to be America. I had had some successes in Paris, but we never considered France. It was Israel or America. And yet, despite everything that had happened, it wasn't easy for me to leave Germany. One afternoon after the radio had announced that I was emigrating to the United States, I was in my room playing the piano when Frau Feinstiehl, our elderly German housekeeper, knocked on the door and announced, "There's an older man at the front door. He looks pretty nice. He wants to talk to you."

Through the open door I could see that the man was nicely dressed. When he saw me, he said, "Could I please come in? I'd like to talk to you."

"Sure," I said, "come on in."

"Mr. Filar, I heard on the radio that you are emigrating to the United States. Please reconsider. I have my office in Frankfurt here, and at five o'clock I walk home. I hear you when you play the piano in the late afternoon. There's a big tree in front of your house, and I always stop at the tree and listen for about a half hour before I go home. It's almost a ritual with me. I know we did horrible things to you during the war, but it's different now. We would love to have you stay in Germany. Please stay." What could I say?

At one of my last meetings with Mr. Gieseking, I asked him what I should do. I was still looking for advice from everyone. I was afraid to go to the States because I didn't know anybody and I didn't know the language. Mr. Gieseking encouraged me to go. "Germany is in ruins right now," he said, "and it is going to take quite a few years to get it rebuilt. In America everything is normal and going strong. I believe you'll have a great career there. Go."

Once more he gave me a beautiful letter of recommendation to use in America. I have it framed and hanging on the wall next to my piano:

To whom it may concern:
This is to recommend Mr. Marian Filar, whose pianistic and artistic development I was able to watch very closely since 1946. In my opinion Mr. Filar has a musical talent of absolutely exceptional qualities. His interpretations, especially of the compositions by Chopin, are among the most perfect and the most beautiful I have ever heard and show a particularly deep feeling and understanding for the works of the great Polish composer. I am happy that I have been able to help Mr. Filar to appear in concerts in France, Portugal, and other European countries. His success was everywhere up to the highest expectations, and I feel therefore sure that Mr. Filar will start in America just as brilliant a career as the one he has initiated in Europe. I hope that the many Americans interested in good music will help Marian Filar to become quickly recognized and appreciated as one of the finest musicians among pianists.

Walter Gieseking
February 1950

He also told me, "Don't worry about defending me when you get to America. I can take care of myself. You have a career to start. Look after *you*. Don't worry about me." We continued to correspond until his death in 1956, and I have letters and cards from him from all over the world. And of course we saw each other whenever our concert paths crossed in Europe or America.

Once our decision was made, my brothers and I packed everything up, and I shipped my piano to the States. When the day to leave finally arrived and the truck came to take our things away, Frau Feinstiehl was at the window with a kitchen towel in her hand—she always carried a kitchen towel. When the movers came in, she said, "Now it's getting serious!" and started to cry bitter tears. I think she thought maybe we'd change our minds. She was very attached to us, and she especially loved me. When I had unexpected guests, all of a sudden cookies she had just made would appear on the table. Or when I would say, "Where's my shirt that was hanging up?" she would say, "It's in the drawer." She had washed and pressed it and put it away. She was an older woman, but she was full of energy! She took care of the whole apartment so that we had nothing to worry about. Before we left, my brother Michael arranged to get her a job with an American colonel he knew so that she would not be left without means.

Part 5:

New World

Getting Started in a New Land

On the morning of March 3, 1950, I had my first sighting of the silhouetted skyline of New York City. After a rough, ten-day-long, winter passage, the American military transport ship *General Greeley* was delivering its cargo of DPs to the United States. I was on deck excitedly waiting for my first view of the most beautiful statue in all the world, the Statue of Liberty. As we approached it, I strained to take it all in, every detail of its face and form:

> Give me your tired, your poor,
> Your huddled masses yearning to breathe free,
> The wretched refuse of your teeming shore.
> Send these, the homeless, tempest-tost to me,
> I lift my lamp beside the golden door!

I couldn't read English, of course, but the sight of the statue welcoming us sent tears streaming down my face.

We docked at the Fifty-seventh Street Pier in Manhattan. A few minutes later newspaper reporters came swarming on board. Somebody had told them a concert pianist was on the ship, so they gathered around to ask me questions. The only English I knew was "Okay" and "I love you," which I had learned from American movies. One of the reporters who understood German acted as translator.

"How do you like America?" was the first question. And I hadn't even gotten off the boat!

"How do you like China?" I answered.

"I've never been in China," the reporter said.

"I've never been in America," I snapped back. "I'm excited to be here, but now why not ask me about something I know."

Joel looked at me with disgust. "There you go with your big mouth! You're already starting out on the wrong foot." I admit I was a little impatient with the reporters, but it was only seven o'clock in the morning, and a lot of us, including me, were still pretty sick from the rough voyage.

One of the reporters grabbed a little girl, put her on top of the ship's upright piano, and asked me to sit down and smile for a photo. "Show teeth," he said and took a "spontaneous" picture. That was my first experience with the New York press.

When the representatives of a refugee organization finally arrived, they bundled us into cars to take us to a DP hotel. As the car zoomed along the West Side Highway, I said to Michael in amazement, "Look at this! They don't have sidewalks? What's going on? Nobody walks here?" When we turned off at Seventy-second and reached Broadway, I relaxed. "Oh, thank goodness," I said. "This looks *normal*." I could see people walking around on sidewalks, so I felt better.

We didn't have to stay at the DP hotel very long since luckily Joel had enough money saved that we could rent an apartment in Woodside, Queens. It had three small bedrooms and a living room. And after my piano arrived, I was able to practice once again.

How does a European concert pianist restart his career in America? The way any other displaced person does—by learning English. Before Carmel Offie had returned to the States, he had told me, "When you go to America, I'll be able to help you. I'll introduce you to Ambassador Bullitt. He'll get you an audition with Eugene Ormandy. If those two like you, you'll do okay. But first you have to learn English." So that's exactly what I set out to do.

For eight months my brothers and I took high school night classes in English for new arrivals. There were about thirty of us in the class, opinionated immigrants from all the countries of Europe, always arguing with each other. I remember how our teacher, an African American, would get exasperated with us. "Hey! The war's over! Settle down and start behaving. This is America. We don't fight here." Another thing he told us: "Don't buy the *New York Daily News*. If you want to learn English, read the *New York Times*."

Small incidents from that first year in New York were turning points in my becoming an American. One night in late December Michael and I were walking home on Queens Boulevard when we passed a little produce store selling grapes. "Look!" I said. "Grapes in December! Let's buy a pound." But when I took a closer look at the grapes and noticed little fruit flies flitting around them, the fruit was suddenly less attractive. When the grocer approached, I asked him if I could buy just a quarter pound.

"Yeah, sure," he said sarcastically. "And how many bags do you want for your quarter pound?"

"I don't want any free bags," I shot back, "and I don't want any free flies either."

When we got home I announced to Joel and Michael, "Let's have a drink! I finally was able to talk back to a New Yorker!" That felt great!

Another incident a little later convinced me that I was on my way to speaking English like a native. After I started going out and playing the piano at parties at the homes of people who had an interest in classical music, I decided it was time for me to buy a nice suit. So I went to Broadstreet's at Fifth Avenue and Forty-seventh to pick a suit out. I entered the store and walked around for the longest time without anyone offering to help me. People came in after me, bought clothes, and left and still nobody approached me. Although my suit was a fine European cut, tailored to my specifications in Frankfurt after three fittings, I guess it must have been obvious that I was a European DP, and everyone knew that DPs didn't have a cent. They just came into stores to look.

Finally, a salesman sauntered over to me and in a tough New York tone said, "Whadda ya want?"

"I want to buy an elephant. Ya got one?" I said in the same tone.

"Hey, you speak English! What can I do for you?"

"Now that you sound civilized, maybe I'll buy a suit." And I did, my first off-the-rack American-style suit. When I got home, my brothers and I again celebrated our most recent step to becoming New Yorkers.

I spent the rest of 1950 mostly studying English, practicing on my wonderful old Steinway, and meeting members of New York's musical world. I also began going to concerts at Carnegie Hall. That brings me back to the question of how a European classical pianist restarts his career in America. Good luck and old friends have a lot to do with it. And sometimes enemies, too.

When I had been in the United States only a month or two, I managed to get an appointment to see André Mertens, vice president of Columbia Artists. There were two big artist-management firms at the time, Columbia Artists and the National Concert Artists Corporation. I arrived on time at Mr. Mertens's Fifty-seventh Street office, only to be kept waiting for an hour. Since Mertens was a Jewish fellow from Vienna, when I finally did meet him, I asked if we could speak German. "Mr. Mertens," I said, "I've been here only a couple of months and I'm still learning English. Do you mind if we speak German?" He answered me with a string of incomprehensible English words. "I'm sorry, Mr. Mertens," I replied in German, "I can't understand you. Can we speak German?"

"Oh, you understand. You understand," he said. But I didn't.

As we played verbal ping-pong in English and German, I tried to catch his meanings. But he made a monkey out of me, ignoring my every attempt to communicate. It was horrible. Finally, I had to get up and leave his office. I remember crying on the way down in the elevator. What was that all about? What had I done to deserve such treatment?

I also mentioned good luck and old friends. One night at Carnegie Hall in April 1950 I met a former colleague of mine from the Conservatory in Lemberg—we had graduated at the same time. He was with a friend of his whose name was Mr. Kosches, a pianist who had been in the United States for many years. As we were leaving, Mr. Kosches said to me, "I am playing chamber music next Sunday with Misha Mishakoff, the concertmaster of Toscanini's NBC orchestra. Why don't you come with me? I'm sure you will meet someone of interest there. It might be a good opportunity for you."

So I went and met Mr. Mishakoff, and afterward I had a wonderful time playing piano-violin sonatas with him. He liked my playing tremendously and at one point said to me, "Do you know Franco Autori? No? He's the associate conductor of the New York Philharmonic, the right-hand man of Dimitri Mitropoulos. He's also the conductor for the summer concerts in Chautauqua, New York. He married a Polish woman from Warsaw, a pianist, I believe. I think she studied at the Conservatory in Warsaw. You may know her. If you want, I'll give you her phone number."

"Sure. Do you know her maiden name?"

"Its *zhib zhib zhib*." He couldn't pronounce Polish names, so I didn't have a clue who she might be. A few days later, when I was in Manhattan, I decided to call her from a phone booth. Autori answered the phone. "What did you say your name was? Pilar? Silar?"

In the background I heard a woman's voice shout, "Filar! Let me talk to him!" She must have yanked the phone out of his hand. "Marian Filar, is that you?"

"Yes, it is. And who is this?"

"It's Lilka Berezynska!"

Lilka! My old classmate! We hadn't seen each other in eleven years—since 1939.

I took a bus over to their apartment on West Seventy-first. It was a great reunion with Lilka, and her husband couldn't have been warmer toward me. He knew I had studied with Mr. Gieseking, so Lilka had obviously told him all about me. She must have pushed to have him add me to the Chautauqua concert schedule because he made a point of explaining that the schedule had already been set.

"Sure, I understand," I said. "There's always next year. I didn't come here as a tourist, after all. I came to stay." I had a glass of wine and was content just being reunited with Lilka and making a new friend. At one point in the evening Autori asked me to play something. So I sat down at his piano and played the Tchaikovsky concerto. As I finished the first movement, or maybe before, he stopped me and pulled out his schedule for the summer Chautauqua season. "Do you see this last concert listing? We've talked to the singer, but we haven't signed the contract yet. So look what I'm doing." He crossed out the singer's name and put in mine. That's how I got my first concert in the United States. It was in Chautauqua in western New York state, and about ten thousand people attended. It was quite a success, with excellent reviews that helped get me off on the right foot in America.

In the late summer of 1950 I received a call from my friend Carmel Offie, letting me know he had arranged an audition for me with Eugene Ormandy, the conductor of the Philadelphia Orchestra. So I went to Philadelphia for the audition, which took place in Ormandy's apartment in the Bellevue Stratford Hotel. We spoke German since my English was still not very good and because Ormandy was originally from Hungary and spoke German fluently. I had been told in Europe that if you wanted to play with a great symphony orchestra in the United States, you had to tell them with whom you had played in Europe. If you had only played with a hole-in-the-wall orchestra, they wouldn't engage you. So I began my meeting with Ormandy by mentioning the orchestras I had performed with and then offered to show him my reviews.

"I don't have to see anything! Don't you think I know something about music? Come on, sit down and *play!*"

I thought, "What kind of character is this?" Maybe I was hoping for someone like Hermann Abendroth, who had been so pleasant and warm to me at our first meeting. "Tell me how you want to play the Chopin," he had said. "I want to accompany you so you'll have a great success." The feeling I got from Ormandy was quite different. I played for him about ten minutes, and then he stopped me. "Okay. You'll hear from me." That was it. So I figured it hadn't worked out and went home to Queens.

I found out later that he had just divorced his first wife and had been in a hurry to catch a plane to Europe, which might have had something to do with the way he treated me. Three weeks later I received a letter from him: "I am preparing Beethoven's Ninth Symphony for a performance in three months. Do you know his Choral Fantasie for Piano, Chorus, Vocal Soloists, and Orchestra, Op. 80? If so, I will add it to the program for four performances."

Agh! What bad luck! I knew so many piano concertos, and here was Ormandy offering me something I didn't know. There were no recordings of it, and no place to hear it. I had heard it performed only once, years before in Frankfurt, when my friend Heinz Schroeter played it with the State Radio Orchestra. It is not an easy piece. There are a lot of entrances, a lot of waiting as the soloist or the choir sings, and it can get quite complicated. To make matters worse, when Ormandy sent me the music, his tempo signs seemed a bit too fast. I considered not accepting the engagement, but a friend, Irving Gelford, who had studied composition at Juilliard, set me straight. "You aren't going to accept Ormandy's offer?" he shouted. "Are you crazy? People wait a lifetime for a break like this, and it never comes. And he's even going to pay you! Sit down and start digging in."

Irv was a great friend, writing letters for me until two in the morning before I learned English. He owned a beautiful house outside of New York on six acres of land in Suffern. We used to call it Grand Central Station because he'd regularly invite fifty or sixty people out there for Sunday cookouts. He was a true music lover who was never able to fulfill his dream of becoming an accomplished composer because of family responsibilities. I knew Irv was right, so I notified Ormandy I'd do it.

I also sent Ormandy's tempo markings to Gieseking for his opinion. He wrote back, "Yes, this is a little fast, but in America everything is a little faster. They drive faster, they live faster, they play faster, and now they even talk faster. And if you want to play with Ormandy again, you'd better listen to him." That seemed like very sound advice. The truth is, I never knew Mr. Gieseking *not* to give good advice. So I got down to business and learned the piece in three months.

The first performance was on a Friday afternoon, a matinee when the famous blue-rinse set, as they called the older ladies who came in from the suburbs to go shopping and have lunch and then go over to the Academy of Music for a little culture. I played the piece, but after I finished my performance, I couldn't help thinking that the applause had been tepid. In the green room I said to Ormandy. "I'm sorry, Maestro. I guess the audience didn't like me. The applause was so weak."

"What are you talking about? That was sensational applause. Those ladies are old and tired. When they clap twice, they've had it. And they clapped maybe twenty times. They loved you!" Ormandy was definitely pleased and reengaged me on the spot for the following year.

Mr. Offie convinced me to join the musicians' union in New York, Local 802. In Europe no artist belonged to a union, but Mr. Offie said I had to join or I would not be able to play with symphony orchestras in America. It wasn't easy to get into the union, but Mr. Offie knew some people and when the time came went with me to the union office. When I had to pay a fifty-dollar entrance fee, I asked the fellow as he gave me a receipt, "What does the union do for the fifty dollars?"

"Oh, we just take your money," he said. At the time his answer really upset me, but after I became Americanized, I realized he was just trying to be funny.

In the meantime, as my English continued to improve, Mr. Offie invited me to Washington, D.C., to play at a dinner party at the home of his boss, Ambassador Bullitt. There were many important guests there—generals and admirals, Poland's ambassador to Berlin before the war, Joseph Lipski, and the Washington legend, the very impressive Alice Roosevelt Longworth, daughter of President Theodore Roosevelt. That evening, after everyone left, Ambassador Bullitt invited me to be his houseguest for the week.

What a fantastic experience that was! I was pinching myself in disbelief at my good fortune. Mr. Bullitt was one of the most extraordinary men I've met in my life, incredibly well informed about so many facets of life, including music. We had breakfast together and sometimes lunch. When he wouldn't be home for lunch, I'd get lost in his library or play his beautiful Steinway. While I was there, Mrs. Longworth invited me to her house on Massachusetts Avenue, and I went and played Chopin for her.

Ambassador Bullitt took an interest in my career and introduced me to influential members of Washington society. The ambassador also arranged an audition for me with Howard Mitchell, the conductor of the National Symphony. After I played for Mr. Mitchell, he engaged me, and I played the Chopin E Minor Concerto in Constitution Hall for an audience of five thousand people. I also played a recital at the National Gallery of Art, followed by a second concert with the National Symphony at which I played Beethoven's Third Piano Concerto. As I commuted back and forth between

New York and the nation's capital, I really began to love Washington. What a beautiful city!

About this same time I made my first American recordings. A former colleague of mine from Poland had started a little recording company called Colosseum. He didn't have much money—hardly enough to rent a piano—but we made two recordings in 1951, and they received fantastic write-ups. On the first record I recorded the Chopin Sonata in B Minor, Op. 58, along with four preludes and an étude in B-flat Minor by the Polish composer Karol Szymanowski. The second recording was of eight Chopin nocturnes and a theme and variations by Brzezinski. Later that year a music magazine put both records on its list of the year's ten best classical recordings.

Although I was performing and recording, I still wanted to study. Artur Schnabel, who was one of the foremost interpreters of Beethoven and had edited all of Beethoven's piano sonatas, was based in New York at that time. I had heard his recital at Hunter College, so I called him up—he was listed in the phone book—and introduced myself. I explained that I had played the Choral Fantasie with Mr. Ormandy conducting and wanted to study Beethoven with Mr. Schnabel. He was very nice, but he said that if I had already played the Choral Fantasie with Ormandy, I certainly didn't need to study with him. I tried to change his mind, but I failed. Years later, when I played a concert conducted by Leon Fleischer, who had been a pupil of Schnabel, I told him about the phone conversation. Fleischer told me that when I talked to Mr. Schnabel, he was quite ill and very feeble and was not teaching at all.

Managing without a Manager

My Carnegie Hall debut with the Philadelphia Orchestra on New Year's Day 1952 was a great success. I played the Chopin F Minor Second Concerto to thunderous applause, and with my brothers and friends in attendance, it was truly a wonderful moment in my life. Afterward Ormandy complimented me effusively, and all the critics praised my performance. The only thing missing from my New York debut was the presence of a single classical music manager. Not a single one came. Sol Hurok had seen to that.

The week after my successful Carnegie Hall debut I went to see the president of the National Concert Artists Corporation, Marks Levine, to see about getting placed under their management. "Mr. Filar," he said as I walked into his office, "I know all about you. You don't need a manager, do you? You're already getting better concerts than I can get for my pianists. And you're saving money. You don't pay anybody any commission."

"It's not so, Mr. Levine. Yes, I've known some people from Europe who have arranged auditions for me. The conductors like me, so I play, but I can't be my own manager. Why don't you take me on? Whatever your fee is, I'll gladly pay it."

"Oh, no, no. You don't need a manager, Mr. Filar. You don't need a manager." I got absolutely nowhere. I did not know then that Sol Hurok had a stranglehold on the musical world in America in the 1950s, and apparently I was on his blacklist. My crime was that I had studied with Gieseking, and not being in Frankfurt to meet Hurok when he called had not helped. I tried to reach him to explain, but each time I called his office and mentioned my name, his secretary gave me the brush-off. She might as well have said, "Mr. Filar, Mr. Hurok is vacationing on the moon." I finally realized I was wasting my time trying to explain anything to Sol Hurok.

I later went to hear a recital of Arthur Rubinstein at Carnegie Hall and then went backstage to meet him. I introduced myself, speaking in Polish: "Mr. Rubinstein, I played for you in Warsaw when I was ten years old. I'm sure you don't remember."

"As a matter of fact, I don't."

"I can refresh your memory. I'll tell you where it was exactly. I'll describe the street and the house."

"Go ahead."

I did.

"Hey, you're right. I remember you now! I'm staying at the Essex Hotel. Come by and see me."

So I went to the Essex, where he had a piano, and played for him. "Oh, I can do a lot for you," he said, but I don't think he realized the situation. About a year later, while I was visiting with him in the green room after another one of his recitals, Hurok walked in. Arthur pointed to me and asked Hurok directly why he wouldn't take me on. "Why not present him, Sol? He's a wonderful artist."

Hurok put on a sour face and without answering turned and walked out of the room.

Rubinstein and I remained personal friends and had great times together whenever we met. He was a great talker, and I think he liked to take a break from English and speak Polish with me. Once it got me in a little trouble. At a reception that Fred Mann, a Phila-delphia-based concert producer, gave for Rubinstein in Philadelphia after one of his concerts, Rubinstein grabbed me and sat me down on a sofa for a chat. "I'm tired of all that English," he told me.

Rubinstein sat with his back to the party, and we talked for an hour and a half. We were having a great time, but from where I was sitting I could see that Fred was getting more and more upset be-cause Rubinstein was talking exclusively to me and forgetting all the guests who had come to meet him. But what could I do? Tell Rubinstein to stop talking?

About two in the morning Fred's maid brought him the morning paper. As a joke, Fred brought it to Rubinstein and said, "There is a bad write-up in here about the concert, Arthur." Rubinstein's face instantly turned as white as a sheet of paper. Everything about him changed.

"No, no," I quickly interjected, "Fred's just pulling your leg." But that was how concerned Rubinstein was with what critics said.

Critics—what can I say? They are a necessary evil? I prefer the term *reviewers*. Unfortunately, few of them are as educated as Pro-fessor Drzewiecki was. When he wrote a review, he really knew what he was talking about. I have consistently received wonderful reviews, but I take them all with a grain of salt. I know when I play well. I don't need someone else to tell me. And some of the review-ers just don't know what they're talking about.

The music critic for the *Philadelphia Inquirer* once told me that his predecessor, as he started to get old, used to write his reviews the day before the concert so that he could go to bed early. I'm sure he must have had a problem when I made my debut with the

Philadelphia Orchestra. With my first name, he would have had to show up just to find out if I was male or female.

When it came to sociability, how different Vladimir Horowitz was from Rubinstein. If it was hard for Rubinstein to stop talking, it was hard to get Horowitz to begin. Everything Horowitz managed to say, he said in a dull monotone. However, he was a wonderful pianist, especially when he played the Russians. He was especially good with Scriabin and Rachmaninoff. However, he wasn't that great when it came to Chopin. But, as Professor Drzewiecki used to say, "Nobody can murder Chopin." That's because Chopin's music is so beautiful that audiences love to hear it no matter how poorly it's played.

One of my favorite jokes is about a pianist who plays a Chopin concert in Paris. He is really terrible. And yet as he finishes the piece, the entire audience starts screaming, "Encore! Encore!" So he plays it again, and he's even worse, if that's possible. But again the audience is on its feet, screaming, "Encore! Encore!" And he's thinking, "Wow, they really love me. I guess I'll play it again." And as he sits down and everyone is still yelling "Encore!" he hears someone in the balcony shout, "If you play it enough times, maybe you'll finally get it right!"

I continued to concertize in the United States and abroad, thanks to my contacts, since Sol Hurok wasn't about to help. Some of what happened behind the scenes at these concerts may be of interest and shed some light on America's classical music scene, especially in the 1950s, when America's symphonies were establishing their worldwide reputations.

In 1952 I was soloist with the Chicago Symphony, conducted by my friend from Prague, Rafael Kubelik. It came about this way: I was reading the newspaper in New York one morning and saw that he was conducting in Chicago. I called the Chicago Symphony and asked, "Is Mr. Kubelik actually in town now? I mean, he's not going anywhere, is he? I want to come to his concert!" Then I took a plane to Chicago. The next morning I got up early and went over to the orchestra hall on Michigan Avenue. When I told his secretary that I wanted to see Mr. Kubelik, she asked me if I had an appointment. "No," I said, "but please give him my card." A moment later he came flying out of his office and wrapped me in a bear hug: "Filar, what are you doing in Chicago?" I said, "I came to see you, what else?" We had lunch together and had a wonderful time. He offered me an engagement for the next year to play the Chopin E Minor Concerto.

However, when I went to Chicago the following year, the old problem of my having to play an unfamiliar piano came back to haunt me in a most distressing way. When I arrived, I discovered that the official piano of the Chicago Symphony was a Baldwin. All U.S. orchestras adopted an official piano, and if you wanted to play on stage with them, you usually had to play that piano. However, I wasn't used to a Baldwin—I was a Steinway artist. When I explained my situation, they arranged for me to have a Steinway piano to play.

At the first rehearsal, as I started to play, I noticed that my piano sounded off. While the orchestra was tuning its A at 444 vibrations per second, my Steinway was tuned to the normal A, which is 440 vibrations per second. The orchestra wanted to sound a little higher and more brilliant, but because I was lower, I sounded dead, as if my piano were almost one quarter tone lower.

After the rehearsal was finished, I went over to Mr. Kubelik. Of course, he was my friend, and I didn't want to create a problem for him, but I was stuck. What could I do? I tried to be diplomatic. When I told him about my concern, he assured me, "Don't worry about it. We'll tune your piano tonight." Then I went straight to the Steinway dealer on Wabash Avenue to ask its store manager why he hadn't tuned the piano to 444 when it was delivered to the Chicago Symphony. That's when I walked right into the middle of a big, fat quarrel between Steinway and the symphony, which I knew nothing about.

The manager was incensed. "No! We're not going to ruin our

pianos. If they want to sound more brilliant, that's their problem, but we're tuning our pianos to 440, period. If Baldwin wants to tune up to 444, they can, but we will not. And that's final!"

"I didn't come here to fight," I told him. "I came here to play a concert, and I'd like to make it a success. But I sound dead when I play with the orchestra that high."

"Talk to the conductor! We have nothing to do with it. We are not going to pull the A up to 444 and ruin our pianos. Forget it!"

He was in a fighting mood, and there I was in the middle of it. "Nice career," I thought. "First I can't get a manager, and then I come here and get in the middle of a war between piano companies. I might as well go back to Europe. This is awful."

But Mr. Kubelik had said not to worry about it, that they would tune the piano themselves, and I trusted him. The night of the concert, when I came on stage early to sound the A, the concert-master said to me, "Don't bother to sound the A, it's all right. It's been tuned." I believed him, so I didn't sound the A. If I had, I wouldn't have played.

When the orchestra started the introduction, and I started to play—and I do have perfect pitch—I still sounded dead. They hadn't tuned the piano, and they hadn't tuned down the orchestra either. It was the same as before, and I was in big trouble. I thought, "They lied! That's dirty. I'm going to lay a huge egg here. This is going to be the end of me." I felt myself getting angry, so when I finished the first movement, I started to hit the A a number of times to try to tune the orchestra, because I sure as hell couldn't tune the piano. I didn't know what else to do. I wanted to jump right out the window, it sounded so bad. So they pretended to tune a little, but actually they didn't do a damn thing.

The next morning the headline was "Pianist Sounds A, Conductor Sounds Off!" I was appalled and immediately apologized profusely to Mr. Kubelik. He was a wonderful friend whom I loved dearly, and I certainly didn't want him to get any bad press. "Don't worry about it," he said. "We'll play again next year, and everything will be okay." And we did play again the following year, and, as he promised, everything was fine, and we both received beautiful reviews.

That was my first experience with the idea of an "official" piano, but it was by no means the last. When I was invited to play in Philadelphia, the official piano of the Philadelphia Orchestra at the time was the Lester. I couldn't understand it. As a new American, I was asking, "What's an official piano anyway? Do they have official trumpets, too? Why just an official piano?" In Philadelphia if you didn't want to play the Lester, you didn't have to. You could hire your own piano, but you had to pay for it. On the program the Lester would still be listed as the "official piano of the Philadelphia Orchestra."

Once when I was invited to dinner at the home of the president of the board of the Philadelphia Orchestra, Orville Bullitt, the brother of Ambassador Bullitt, I asked, "Mr. Bullitt, what does this mean, an official piano? Is there an official flute or an official double bass or an official bow?" He said, "It's a gimmick. Years ago the orchestras started to adopt pianos because the manufacturers wanted to have some publicity and liked the endorsements of orchestras. At that time I talked to Mr. Ormandy about it, and he said, 'Of course, it will have to be the Steinway.'

" 'Hey, wait a minute,' I said to him. 'I've talked to Steinway, and they'll give us a piano, sure, but they won't pay us anything. Lester offered us fifty thousand dollars a year! Since I have a budget to worry about, I have to accept their offer.'

"But Ormandy insisted, 'It has to be the Steinway.' So I said to him, 'Okay, Eugene, let's put it to a test. I'll place the two pianos on the stage—a concert Steinway and a concert Lester—and then we'll go out in the audience and turn our backs to the stage and ask a pianist to play the same short piece on both pianos. If you can tell the difference, it's going to be the Steinway; otherwise it's going to be the Lester.'

"So we went over to the academy one morning, and a pianist

came out and played first on one piano then on the other. When he finished, I said to Eugene, 'Okay, which is which?' and Ormandy said, 'I can't tell.' So I said, 'Okay, it's going to be the Lester and fifty thousand dollars for the Philadelphia Orchestra.' " So that's how the Lester became the "official" piano of the Philadelphia Orchestra.

In 1953 I toured mostly outside the United States, making the first of several tours to Scandinavia, Mexico, and South America. In Denmark I played with the conductor Eric Tuxen, a marvelous giant of a man and a great conductor. When I played with Eric and the Danish Symphony that first time, I got twelve rave reviews and one big fat nasty knock from the communist paper. It began, "The Americanized Polish pianist Marian Filar . . ." I showed it to Eric: "Look at this, twelve raves and this one pans me!" Eric gave it a glance and said, "That's the way it should be. If you had gotten a rave from them, we would have been suspicious. This is legitimate—otherwise we would have thought you were a communist. They automatically cut up anyone who is not a member of the party."

In South America I played concerts conducted by Igor Markevitch, a great conductor and a student of Nadia Boulanger, who also taught Leonard Bernstein; Vladimir Golschmann, who at the time was conductor of the St. Louis Symphony; and Eleazar de Carvalho, conductor of Brazil's Symphonia del Estado.

Playing with Mr. Markevitch was quite an experience. We started the concert at the time most concerts are ending—at 10:30 at night. In Buenos Aires people eat a late dinner and then go to a concert. And they don't worry very much about being on time. They just stroll in whenever they please. Mr. Markevitch opened the program and conducted an overture, and he still was forced to stand and wait on stage while people walked in late. When I came out from the wings to begin the concerto with him, people were still ambling in through all the doors. He just turned around and glared at them. He was so mad, he was swearing at them under his breath. I was sitting right there, so I heard every word. What a night! Here it was eleven o'clock, you come out on stage to begin your concert, the audience is still sauntering in without a care in the world, and your conductor is swearing at them right next to you! Once we got going, though, we managed to make pretty good music.

In Buenos Aires I also played a recital at the Teatro Colon, which is the most famous opera theater in all of South America and a truly interesting building. Here they built special boxes just for mourners. When a member of the family dies, it is thought to be unseemly for the rest of the family to go out in public or be seen at an amusement, so boxes were built beneath the floor of the orchestra with concrete benches along the walls and bars across the windows. There are separate entrances, and nobody can see in. When the mourners look out, all they can see are people's legs. The mourners don't get to see much of anything, but at least they get to hear the music. So, the members of the family in mourning walk in unobserved, walk out, get in the car, and drive off, not mingling with anybody. Officially, they were never in public, but they still could listen to the music, which I thought was a beautiful idea.

After the concert, when everyone had finished offering congratulations and getting autographs, I went to get my wraps. There was a guard sitting in the little cubicle where I had left them. I picked up my coat and went to get my scarf and gloves, but they were gone. I looked at the guard and said, "I had a scarf and gloves here."

He smiled. "Well that's a good sign! It means you are very popular."

"It does?"

"Oh yes. The young girls who are always at these concerts go around and steal small items of clothing when they like you, and then they say to each other, "I have a souvenir of this one and that one. I have so-and-so's scarf or so-and-so's hat.' They steal all sorts of things when they like you. If they didn't take anything, it means you weren't much of a success."

"Oh, great," I said, "next time I'll bring a basket full of extra clothes."

"Yeah," he said and smiled, "that would be a good idea."

When I played my concert in São Paulo, I met Sarah, a wonderful woman whom I eventually married. But the marriage did not last because we couldn't agree about where to live. She tried to live in Philadelphia, but she didn't like it. She tried to convince me to move to Brazil, but I said, "No, you live here. I'm not going to live in Brazil. This is my country, this is my life." So we parted as friends, and we are still friends.

Professor Drzewiecki once told me something I've never forgotten. He was married, but he told me, "You are married to the piano for the rest of your life. It will give you pleasure as long as you live. It will never talk back to you, never divorce you or fight with you. It's the greatest friend that you are going to have." It's so true. I'm divorced but not from the piano. I was married to the piano when I was four years old and have been ever since. I love it and always will.

He also said that you can release all your emotions into the beauty of the piano's sound. And that's true, too. Pianists can have disappointments in love, but when you sit down at the piano and pour your heart out, your friend does whatever you need it to do so that you can be healed. When I sit down at the piano, I feel I am in heaven. I close my eyes, and I'm playing for my mother. I think she's sitting next to me. Or my sister Helen, or my brother. I'm in a different mood, back in the world of my wonderful childhood, back before all hell broke loose.

Settling Down

When I returned from concerts in South America in 1953, I began taking stock of my situation. I had been in the United States three years, and was, as they say, getting by. The pay wasn't bad for those days, but not great—about two hundred dollars for a performance. I began to tell myself that I had to start making a *real* living. Since everybody seemed to be teaching at that time—Rudolf Serkin was teaching, this one and that one was teaching, many of the big names of the day—I began to think about finding a teaching position. And I found it in September 1953 when the Settlement Music School in Philadelphia offered me a job as the head of its piano department. The Curtis Music Institute was an outgrowth of the Settlement Music School.

It was a wonderful position, and I loved it. I taught piano to the most eager, talented young boys and girls I could ever have hoped for, ages ten to seventeen. The school had never had any of its students win the Philadelphia Orchestra's Youth Contest, and during my first year there we had our first winner. All in all, about ten of my students went on to play with the Philadelphia Orchestra. The board jumped for joy when two of them, Charles Birenbaum, playing the Chopin E Minor Concerto, and Beth Levine, performing Beethoven's Third Piano Concerto, beat out Curtis Music Institute students in the Philadelphia Orchestra competition.

One of my most interesting students at the Settlement Music School was Marcia, who came to me when she was about eleven years old. When she arrived with her mother for the audition, her mother was carrying a piano music stand. When I asked her what it was for, she said, "We clip it onto the piano stand because Marcia doesn't see too well." She had been born prematurely, and when they put her in an incubator, they gave her too much oxygen. As a result, she was blind in one eye and had only about 20 percent vision in the other. She sat at the piano with her little belly almost on the keyboard and her nose in the music. All she could do then was bang the keys. I thought, "Oh boy, what do I do now?"

I decided to test her eyes, so I stood back and said, "Marcia, how many fingers do you see?" She said, "Three." I said, "Very good." I had held up two. She couldn't see worth beans. And yet she was so burning with desire to play the piano, I never saw anything like it. Her eagerness was contagious. I'll never forget it. I tested her ear, and she had perfect pitch. So there was something there all right. I thought for a minute and then said, "Look, I don't have an opening right now." It was December before the holidays. "But at Christmas, I have somebody leaving for California, so I'll have one opening. I'll take you for four weeks as an experiment. And I have some ideas. If they work, you can play the piano. Otherwise, give it up. You can't play the way you're playing now. For the next couple weeks just play softly and from memory." I added, "You know, Marcia, when God takes away one of the senses from a human being, He usually gives back more somewhere else, so I'm hoping you have a wonderful memory. If you have, we'll be able to do something together." And as it turned out, her memory was fantastic.

When she came back for her first lesson, I said, "Marcia, from now on, you are going to sit like I sit, and hold your hands on the piano like everybody else. And when you come back next week, I want you to have learned from memory what I am going to give you. You will never have music again on the stand. Forget it. You'll learn your music on the sofa. You'll memorize it, and you'll hear it in your head."

"But how can I do that? It's impossible!"

"Not so fast. You live in an apartment or a house, right? You have your own room? Can you describe it? Where's the window when you go in the door?"

"Straight ahead."

"Where's the bed?"

"To the left."

When I went on asking where's this, where's that, she described the room to the last little detail.

"Do you see it all in your head?"

"Yes."

"That's how you are going to see the music. You are lucky that I studied with the greatest pianist in the world, and he showed the method to me. That's how I can pass it on to you and how you can be a pianist."

She developed her memory and became a sensation. She had real talent. Two musicians from the Philadelphia Orchestra heard about her and didn't believe it, so they came to the Settlement School to check her out for themselves. She was playing a Bach three-part invention, and I said to her, "Marcia, play the second page, the second line, the third measure, and leave out the second voice," and she did it. The two men still didn't believe it.

I told them, "I can see from your faces that you don't believe this. Here's the music, you test her." They did, and she played whatever they asked for. In a little over a year and a half she won a children's contest and played with the Philadelphia Orchestra.

I told Ambassador Bullitt about her, and he was very excited. He said it was a fascinating story. He told the owners of *Readers' Digest*, whom he knew, and they wanted to do a story on her. When I asked Marcia what she thought about the idea, she said, "On one condition."

"What's that?"

"That they don't talk about my eyes."

"What do you mean?"

"The kids in school, they'll know."

"Are you kidding?" I said. "From the first minute that you walked in here, I saw you had trouble with your eyes."

"Then I don't want to do it," she said and started to cry.

I couldn't take it. "Okay, forget it," I said. "Don't worry. No is no."

Marcia went on to teach music in the public schools. She was a remarkable girl who overcame a tremendous handicap because she had a great desire to play.

I taught at the Settlement Music School from 1953 to 1966, commuting from New York until I moved to Philadelphia in 1959. My teaching schedule permitted annual tours and East Coast performances, including one memorable concert in front of twenty thousand people at Philadelphia's Robin Hood Dell, with Erich Leinsdorf conducting.

Once in New York I went into Woolworth's, and they had canaries on sale for something ridiculous like five dollars. I had never had a bird as a pet, so I bought one. I think the cage was five dollars as well. When I went home and walked in the door holding the cage with the canary in it, my brother Michael looked at it and said, "What in the world are you going to do with that?" I said, "I've always wanted a canary! I'm going to call him Pete!" And that ended that discussion. I kept him next to the piano and taught him how to sing. I'd play a trill to coax him, and he soon got the idea. I'd come in and sit down and talk to him. I'd say, "Want some stimulation?" and play a bunch of arpeggios and a trill, and he'd start right up. He was great. He's even on some of my recordings at home. It got to the point that he'd always sing when I played. And

when I got louder, he'd get louder. I guess he thought it was a competition. He was quite a character, a real Caruso!

In 1955 on one of my visits to a hotel in the Catskills, I had
occasion to remember what had happened to my father in Warsaw
seventeen years earlier when that Polish tax official slapped him
with a "tax" of one hundred thousand zlotys. I would often visit the
hotel in Margaretville, New York, called the Homestead, owned by
Leon Sobolewski, an engineer from Poland with a university education who used to build roads and bridges in Poland. Lots of Polish
emigrants went to the hotel—former generals, former diplomats,
former members of Jósef Pilsudski's government, which had gov-
erned Poland before Hitler invaded. We'd down our drinks, I'd play
old Polish folk songs, and everybody would sing and have a good cry
together thinking of the lost homeland and the good old days. It
was a lot of fun.

I owned my first American car at the time, a Plymouth Belvedere
convertible, and one Sunday night Richard Koc, who had been secretary of the treasury under Pilsudski, asked for a ride back to New
York City. I said, "Gladly." About thirty or forty miles away from
the Homestead, when I knew it was too far for him to walk back, I
said to him, "Mr. Secretary, I'd like to tell you a little story. Something that happened to my dad." And I told him exactly what had
happened and what the tax official had said. Mr. Koc got red in the
face.

"I didn't know the guy," Koc said. "He was just some little official. Nothing to do with me."

"He wasn't so little, Mr. Secretary. His office was right across
from yours. It was official policy he was carrying out. Mr. Secretary,
don't you remember Prime Minister Prystor saying, 'We will not
attack the Jews physically, but we will break them economically?' "

He made a very unpleasant face. "Nothing to do with me," he
said. He didn't like what I was saying at all. "Mr. Secretary," I said
very politely, "if you don't like what I'm telling you, I can stop the

car and you can get out and *walk* to New York." My only regret is that my father wasn't in the back seat to hear us.

About this same time I received a letter from Susanne Brockhaus, the wife of the owner of the great German publishing firm of medical books and encyclopedias. We had met through Mr. Gieseking when I was living in Germany, and a friendship had developed after they had heard me play. One day when I had been visiting them, they had a houseguest, Wilhelm Furtwängler, the greatest German conductor. I played for him, and he liked my playing and predicted a fine career. In her letter, Mrs. Brockhaus asked me to learn an hour-long concerto that Furtwängler had just written so that I could premier it the following year at Carnegie Hall. It was an honor, but an honor I had to refuse. I was afraid to touch it. I didn't dare. As I explained to Mrs. Brockhaus, "Here in America they'll destroy me. They'll say, 'First he studied with Gieseking, now he plays with Furtwängler. He likes Nazis!' "

Guess who ended up playing it? Daniel Barenboim. He was from Israel, so it was kosher. If I had done it, they would have chopped my head off. As a friend of mine said to me, "If you want to make a career in America as a concert pianist, you have to be either from the Soviet Union or from Israel." Fortunately, the situation changed and became much fairer.

By the way, I heard Barenboim play when he was fifteen at the Biltmore Hotel in New York. A Jewish organization arranged it, and Dimitri Mitropoulos of the New York Philharmonic was there. Barenboim is a wonderful pianist, but his management pushed him too much. They already had his whole career mapped out, every step planned, when he was still just a kid.

One day after I had been teaching at the Settlement School for a few years, I received a message from the school's director that Danny Kaye was coming by to meet me. He had had dinner with a member of the Philadelphia Orchestra and had heard about me. It was the start of a lot of great times together. Kids (and women) went crazy around Danny Kaye wherever he went, and the Settlement School was no different. After I calmed the kids down, I played for Danny, and then later we had a chance to talk.

"You know, Mr. Kaye," I said, "I know all about you, but I'm sorry to say I've never seen one of your films. I guess I just haven't been in the United States long enough to have seen you on stage, either."

"Oh? Well, I can fix that. I'm doing a one-man show at the Schubert Theater. I'll leave a ticket for you at the box office. You come to the show and come backstage to see me." So I went to see Danny Kaye's stage show. The place was packed. There must have been two thousand people there. Danny met me, and I ended up backstage during the show because he gave me the job of handing him his paraphernalia—cane, hat, and so forth—while he performed. At the intermission, instead of going offstage, Danny went down front to the edge of the stage, sat down, and dangled his legs over the edge. "I want you to do something for me," he told the audience. "Okay?"

"Okay!" everyone shouted back.

"All right. Now I want this third of you to shout 'Hi!' when I give you the sign. Ready? One, two, three, 'Hi!' "

Everyone shouted, "Hi!"

"Great. Now shut up."

I was standing in the wings wondering what was going on.

"Okay. Now this middle third. I want you to shout 'Fee!' Got it? Okay, one, two, three, Fee!"

Everyone shouted "Fee!" I still didn't get it.

"Great. Now shut up. Now this third shout 'Lar!' All right, one, two, three, 'Lar!' " The whole section screamed "Lar!" Everyone was into it by now.

"Great. Now, all together, in order. One, two, three: HI-FEE-LAR!"

Danny looked back at me and gave me a wink as the people shouted, "Hi, Filar!" at the top of their lungs without knowing what it meant.

When he came backstage, he said, "Did you like that? Did you ever have two thousand people yelling out your name? Special, isn't it? You should have seen the trouble I went through in California having them say hello to Piatigorsky!"

I remember the crazy, funny chaos he stirred up the time he dropped by our apartment in Queens. When he knocked on the door, I opened it. He asked me, "Where's the kitchen?" and rushed right past me.

Joel, who had never met him, was in the kitchen with the door closed. Danny barged in and said, "Hi, I'm Danny Kaye. What do you have in your refrigerator?" By this time Joel had picked up the spirit of Danny's little game, so he ran to protect the refrigerator. I'll never forget the sight of Danny tussling with Joel in our kitchen, trying to open the refrigerator door. When Danny managed to force the door open, he stuck his head all the way inside. He then pulled out a piece of chicken, sat down at the table, and ate it. "What's for dessert?" was his next question.

In 1956 I went to Israel for the first time to play with the Israel Philharmonic—twenty concerts in thirty days—and got to see my brother George and sister Lucy for the first time since the war and to meet their families. One of the concerts was a performance for the Israeli army, and the conductor was an army major. At the end of the concert, a female sergeant came up on stage and presented me with a Bible. I shook hands with her and thanked her. I was later criticized because I hadn't kissed her. Leonard Bernstein had been there a few weeks earlier, and when he received his Bible, he kissed the presenter on both cheeks. When I was criticized for not doing the same, I answered that Bernstein's female sergeant must have been a lot prettier.

While I was on tour with the Israel Philharmonic, the Suez Canal crisis erupted with an attack on Israel by the Egyptian army under President Gamal Abdel Nasser. At the time Francesco Molinari Pradelli, who had conducted at the Met in New York, was conducting the Philharmonic. After a brief interruption in the schedule, our performances resumed a few days later. One night in Petach Tikva, after the orchestra played the first piece on the program, I was about to go out on stage when suddenly there was an air-raid alarm and all the lights went out. Molinari Pradelli said, "*Mama mia,* this is war. Let's get out of here!" and ran outside.

Fortunately, my brother George, who had lived in Israel since 1935, was there. "I bet this is a mistake," he said. "The Arabs don't know yet how to fly at night." Amazingly, there was no panic, and everyone remained in their seats. The orchestra manager asked me to go out on stage in the dark and play a few encores. "Encores?" I said. "I didn't play the concerto yet!" Anyway, somebody got a flashlight, and I went out on stage. I addressed the audience: "Because you are such a wonderful public, not running and not giving into panic, I'm going to play for you a little encore, which I dedicate to Gamal Abdel Nasser!" Total silence. I could feel the consternation in the hall. Then I started to play Chopin's Funeral March! Boy, what a reaction that got! The audience gave me standing ovation. A little later the lights came back on, and we performed the whole printed program.

I had a wonderful reunion with George and Lucy and met their families. When I went to Israel two years later—and then every year after that—I would stay with Lucy and her family, and those visits helped me feel I had a home there. In 1987, Lucy, who never fully recovered from her wartime ordeal, died of a heart condition that had first developed in the freezing temperatures and fierce winds of Siberia.

My brother George was already something of a folk hero in Israel. After he went to Palestine at my mother's urging before the war, he joined the Jewish underground and began developing his engineering skills. Then once the war began, he joined the British army in Palestine and became involved in many military exploits and saw lots of action. He was totally fearless and became quite a renowned hero, earning all sorts of decorations, medals, and commendations from the British government.

He received his highest accolades for a very famous adventure when he was in Alexandria with the British forces after a British ship full of ammunition caught fire and was burning in the harbor. If the ship had exploded, it would have wiped out half the city. George had been a yachtsman as well as an athlete, so he knew all about boats. He jumped into a tugboat—alone—and towed the ammunition ship far out into the Mediterranean. He disconnected his tug and returned as fast as possible to the dock. The moment he stepped ashore, the ammunition ship exploded. He saved thousands of lives. Some of his wartime exploits are chronicled in *Winged Dagger: Adventures on Special Service*, by Roy Alexander Farran (London and New York: Arms and Armour Press, 1986). George helped Major Farran escape from a POW camp in Syria.

In addition to my reunion with my brother and sister, I also met Otto and Ludwig Shorr and some other high school colleagues. We had so much to talk about that we sat in the America House until they closed it up at two in the morning. From our class of about thirty Jewish boys, seven or so survived the Holocaust. Otto, who was an engineer in Jerusalem, told me how he lost his father. When Rabbi Shorr went east after the Germans invaded Poland, he got stuck behind the Russian lines, as I did. A Jewish communist pointed him out to the KGB as the chief rabbi of Warsaw, so the Russians grabbed him and killed him. Otto was still trying to find out where his father was buried so he could bring his remains to Jerusalem.

Otto's mother and sister were already buried there. In fact, I went to their graves with Otto. His mother had been in Italy when the Germans captured her and Otto's sister. His mother put a capsule of cyanide into her mouth. When you bite on it, you're dead, but this cyanide was very old, so when his mother bit on it, she didn't die but was only in horrible pain. So his sister gave her mother her capsule, which was newer. The mother took it and died instantly. Then Otto's sister jumped out a window to her own death.

Although I had an incredible time being reunited with family and friends after so many years, not everything was wonderful about that visit to Israel. While I was in Tel Aviv, I received the news that Mr. Gieseking had died. I was heartsick. What a loss for me and for the world. He so loved playing the piano that he always drove himself relentlessly—touring, performing, recording. He had been in London recording Beethoven's thirty-two piano sonatas when suddenly in the middle of a recording session a violent attack of pancreatitis forced him to stop. He was rushed to the hospital, but no one really knew what to do. He was unconscious. Should they operate? There was a fifty-fifty chance of survival. They decided to operate, and he passed away. It was ten days before his sixty-first birthday. Such a shame. He still had so much music left to give.

Just how much he had given me came home two years later, in 1958, when my former teacher, Professor Drzewiecki, came to New York and stayed with us for a few days. When I played some Brahms for him, his eyes popped out of his head. "Where did you learn to play Brahms like that?" he asked. I just looked at him and said, "I only had one teacher after you." Then I played some Mozart, and the professor couldn't believe his ears. There was an enormous difference in my playing since my work with Mr. Gieseking.

Philadelphia

On September 15, 1959, I moved from New York City to Philadelphia to join the music faculty of Temple University. The position that Dr. David Stone, Dean of the College of Music, offered me was ideal. Teaching ten hours a week allowed me to continue with my students—both my Settlement School students and my other private students, who were now coming to me from Philadelphia, Washington, New York, and as far away as Chicago. And Dr. Stone never objected or put obstacles in the way of my continuing my tours and concerts. It was a busy, full life, and Dr. Stone was a wonderful man.

My first apartment was on Rittenhouse Square, right across from the Curtis Institute. I lived in an apartment on the twenty-fourth floor with a magnificent view—you could see all the way to New York City. I later met Joe Scharfsin, who also lived on Rittenhouse Square and who just happened to be Leopold Stokowski's lawyer. When he promised to try to get me an audition with the great man, I was thrilled. He arranged for me to meet Mr. Stokowski in his

New York apartment on Fifth Avenue near the Guggenheim Museum. When I arrived, I found him dressed in an elegant silk dressing gown, European fashion. "What would you like to play for me?" he asked.

"A concerto," I said. For a conductor you don't play a solo piece—that's not smart. They're not really interested in simply how you play. They want to find out if they can play *with* you. I played one movement of the Chopin E Minor Concerto.

"Oh, that's wonderful," he said. "What music would you like to perform with me?" Right off the bat!

"Maestro," I said, "if I had the honor to play with the greatest conductor in the world, I would like to play the Schumann concerto."

He was really surprised at that, "Why the Schumann? Why not Chopin?"

"Because if I play with you, I don't want you just to accompany me, as you would in the Chopin. I want us to make music together, in partnership. That happens in the Schumann. It means I will be making music with one of the greatest musicians of all time. What a great honor and a great pleasure—and what a happy moment it would be for me—to communicate with you musically, instead of just having you accompany me."

He loved my answer. Unfortunately, before we could do a concert together, he died. It would have been an unforgettable experience. I still have a beautiful photo of him that he gave me.

The year 1959 was eventful for another reason. Besides moving to Philadelphia, I went back to Warsaw, which I had not seen since the war. In 1949, when I was still in Germany, I had wanted to enter the very prestigious International Chopin competition in Warsaw, but it was not to be. Mr. Gieseking said I was ready, but the American authorities in Germany told me, "You can do what you want, but we are telling you not to go to Poland. The probability is high that you will be grabbed by the communists. Remember, they can do whatever they want. And if they want you, you're stuck.

Your father was born there, you graduated from school there. To them you're a Polish citizen. To us you're a stateless person, so there will be little we can do to help you if they decide to keep you." I never entered the competition.

However, ten years later it was safe to go because I was now an American citizen, so when I received my invitation to perform with the Warsaw Philharmonic, I went. When I arrived at the airport in Warsaw, Professor Drzewiecki was waiting for me. The first thing he did was warn me, "This is not the same city you knew. Watch out. Don't talk politics. Watch what you say over the phone—everything is bugged." He didn't want me to get into trouble or cause an international incident. "I know," I said. "Don't worry about me."

I stayed in the Hotel Grand, which at that time was one of the best hotels in Warsaw. Former colleagues and friends called to say hello, and every time I picked up the phone, I heard a click. Finally, I got so annoyed that I said into the phone, "Hey, buddy, whatever you want to hear, why don't you ask me. I'll tell you and save you the trouble."

I didn't see much of the city on that trip because of the repressive atmosphere, but I did look for some things. I went to the site of the beautiful old Music Conservatory building, but when I saw nothing there but grass, I cried.

Professor Drzewiecki was with me when I was interviewed by the communist press, which was the only medium the government allowed. During the interview I happened to be holding in my hand a Zippo cigarette lighter, a gift from General Nathan F. Twining, then chairman of the U.S. Joint Chiefs of Staff, whose son was my piano student at the time. A reporter from the communist government newspaper who spotted it asked to see it, so I handed it to him. He inspected it closely and then got red in the face. "This is our enemy!" he shouted. I said, "I know that the general is a friend of the Polish people." The communist government paper printed a nasty review of my concert that began in a familiar way: "The Americanized Polish pianist Marian Filar . . ."

Professor Drzewiecki arranged for me to play Chopin's piano, which is maintained by the Chopin Society in Warsaw. One of Chopin's students, Madame Sterling, had sent the piano from England and signed her name on the sounding board so that no one could switch it. Chopin's piano is a fascinating instrument. It has seventy-seven keys instead of today's eighty-eight. When you play it, you can almost blow on it and the keys will play—that's how light the action is. To our ears Chopin's piano sounds terribly out of tune. If you play an A, you hear an F—a full third below—because they didn't and couldn't pull the A up to 440 vibrations per second, which is the standard tuning today. The entire piano is made of wood, and the sound is very tinny. But Chopin's genius is that he managed to compose music as if he were writing for today's wonderful pianos! He realized that his piano was not the ultimate for the instrument and expressed a wish that some day they would build a sort of piano Stradivarius. He was a double genius, way ahead of his time.

I have also had the privilege of seeing Beethoven's piano. Thanks to Heinz Schroeter's influence when I was in Germany, I was allowed to touch Beethoven's piano keys in the Beethoven Museum in Bonn, which is located in the house where Beethoven was born. His piano was built especially for him by the firm of Konrad Graf in Vienna. Normally there are three strings to a key, starting in the middle and going all the way up. However, Beethoven's piano has four strings per key because he was already going deaf. They figured that if he had a little more sound, he would be able to hear better and longer. It's a very special instrument, and they usually don't let anyone touch it.

When it came time for me to fly from Warsaw to Copenhagen, Denmark, I encountered the communist government one last time at the airport. They checked my U.S. passport at least twenty times, and then when we finally got seated on the plane, the military police came and checked every face and then went to the front of the plane to announce that all the passengers had to spread their legs. They looked under every seat, but they didn't find a single stow-away.

When I arrived in Copenhagen to perform with that beautiful city's symphony orchestra, the first thing I said to the dear friend who was waiting for me was, "How wonderful it is to take a deep breath of free air!"

In 1964 I traded in my old Steinway masterpiece of a piano, which I had purchased in Frankfurt, for a new Steinway B. With a thousand dollars given in trade and 10 percent off for being a Stein-way artist, I paid thirty-seven hundred dollars for the new piano, which is now worth more than fifty thousand dollars. The reason I purchased the new Steinway B is that the older piano had narrower black keys than a modern instrument, and the difference had begun to bother me. So I purchased the newer Steinway to practice and perform on a consistent key width.

My concert tour of Europe in 1965 included performances in Vienna, London, and Paris. While in Paris, I made a pilgrimage to Chopin's grave at the Père-Lachaise cemetery, where many great French writers are also buried. I went with Denise, my cousin's wife. We bought some flowers at a stand outside the cemetery from a lady who told us where the grave was located. She told us that was how she made her living—selling flowers for Chopin's grave.

I brought my Leica camera with me, hoping to take a picture of the grave, but as we went through the entrance, an old guard stopped us and told us that only professional photographers were allowed to take pictures. Denise explained that I was a pianist from America and an interpreter of Chopin's music and that it would mean so much to me if I could take a picture. The guard said that he would permit me to take a picture, but on one condition—that when I got back to New York, I would send him a beautiful postcard of the city. That's all he wanted. I thought to myself that if this had happened in New York, the guy would have said, "Do you have two hundred dollars on you? Otherwise, it's nice knowing you."

We went out and found Chopin's grave, which had flowers placed all around and over it. Every day music lovers and piano students from all over the world come and put flowers on his grave as a tribute, their way of showing their respect and love of Chopin's music. I left my tribute, and we took a picture. As we were leaving, I saw a big, expensive marble monument for Hector Berlioz without a single flower or human being around. When I got back to New York, I sent the guard who let us take the picture one of those oversized postcards of New York—the biggest I could find—with my thanks.

In 1965 I played a recital from hell in Carnegie Hall, something out of one of my worst nightmares. I chose the piano in the Steinway Company's basement across the street, and the workers moved it the next morning to the Carnegie Hall stage. I went to the hall at ten o'clock to hear how it sounded in the recital space. When I sat down and played a little bit, I said to myself, "This can't be the piano I picked!" But then I looked at its number—every piano has a number on the frame—and saw unbelievably that, yes, it was the same piano, except that now it had a little buzzing—not much, but it was there and definitely noticeable. So I called Mr. Hupfer, the chief technician, to tell him the problem and ask him to come over.

He walked in a little while later and looked at me as if he was going to kill me. "Do you know who played that piano two weeks ago?"

"No, who?"

"Sviatoslav Richter!"

"Is that so?" I said. "Then I have a good headline: 'Richter didn't hear it and Filar did!' "

He glared at me and went to the piano. He tried it and heard something too. "Hey! What's that?" he said. He took the whole keyboard out and shook it and shook it and looked under all the hammers before he put it back in, but he couldn't get rid of the buzz, just could not get rid of it. He said to me, "You go sit in the first row and I'll play something and you see if you can hear the buzzing. Then I'll sit in the first row and see if I can hear anything."

So I sat in the first row, and he played a little bit and called out to me, "Can you hear anything?"

I heard it faintly, but maybe in the second or third row they would not be able to hear it at all. So I said, "No, not really." Then we switched places, and he said he couldn't really hear much of anything either.

"Yes," I said, "but I can hear it when I'm playing—and that's what matters."

"Don't worry about it," he said. And that was it. They didn't want to move another piano in and this one out—that cost money. I couldn't do anything about it, so I played the Carnegie Hall recital on a piano with a buzz in it. It was very unsettling, like receiving a little electric shock each time I heard it. Things like can that take your attention off the music and detract from your performance.

After I moved to Philadelphia, I played more dates with the Philadelphia Orchestra and had more contact with Eugene Ormandy and the orchestra's many fine musicians, many of whom became my good friends. Mr. Ormandy was a showman with some set ideas about how things should be done, as I found out when I played the Tchaikovsky piano concerto. At the end of the cadenza of the first movement it has a large run in the right hand. Mr. Ormandy told me to cross over and play the last note, the top note, with my left hand because it looked so much better and sounded better and the audiences loved it! I didn't think so, but I didn't want to offend him. I thought, "He's a violinist, and he's telling me how to play the piano?" However, this was Mr. Ormandy, and I wanted to make sure I kept getting engagements with the orchestra.

During the concert that night I decided that I'd wait and watch Mr. Ormandy to see if he was watching me. When it came time for the run, he was not looking my way, so I played the run as I always did, with just my right hand. As we were leaving the stage, Mr. Ormandy said with a big smile, "Wasn't that great? You sounded terrific playing the way I told you. The audience just went wild!" Naturally, I never let on. Besides, I loved playing with Mr. Ormandy. He was a fantastic accompanist—one of the best. He held your brain in his hand and knew what you were going to do before you did it.

Every cultural organization in this country is always looking for endowments, and the Philadelphia Orchestra was no exception. Many years ago, one of the wealthiest women in Philadelphia asked if she could study with me, and I said yes. She also asked if I would mind coming to her apartment for the lessons since she did not feel right about going to a bachelor's apartment. So I said, "No problem." We both lived on Rittenhouse Square, and all I had to do was walk across the square. She lived in a magnificent apartment that took up the entire eighth floor of the Barclay Hotel, and it had an incredibly gorgeous piano.

She sat down to play for me, and she was almost like a beginner playing the slow movements—terrible. In the course of our lesson she told me that Mr. Ormandy promised her that if she studied with Rudolf Serkin, who was at the Curtis Music Institute, and gave the orchestra one hundred thousand dollars, she could play the Rachmaninoff piano concerto with the Philadelphia Orchestra. Needless to say, she never played with the orchestra, but I don't know how Mr. Ormandy managed to get out of that one! Unless maybe she didn't come up with the money, or he was just daring her.

Sometime during this period I went on a singles' cruise with a friend from New York. We played a lot of ping-pong, but we kept pretty much to ourselves. A girl from Canada who also played ping-pong joined us, and the three of us hung out together. A bunch of women from Brooklyn kept looking us over until they finally came over and said, "What's the matter with you guys? Don't you like women? Why aren't you spending time with us?" I said, "Sure, we like women," and we started talking. They asked us what we did, so I told them we were in business. "What kind of business?" they wanted to know. "We're undertakers," I said, "and I'm president of the company!" They did a U-turn and never bothered us for the rest of the trip.

I have often been invited to be a judge at piano competitions, both in the United States and abroad. One such competition in 1977 was particularly memorable for me. Arthur Rubinstein invited me to be a judge at the Arthur Rubinstein International Master Piano Competition in Tel Aviv and Jerusalem. The jury included a colleague of mine from Warsaw, Jan Ekier, who is now editing all of Chopin's music for publication in a national edition in Poland.

The competition included wonderful, talented pianists, as well as a few who tried to play faster than the speed of sound, which Rubinstein and I didn't like. One fellow in particular played both books of Brahms's Paganini Variations faster than anything I've ever heard. I was sitting next to Rubinstein at that session and could see by the expression on his face how much he disliked it. When the pianist finished, I turned to Rubinstein and said, "Maestro, look! He's taking a bow, and the keys are still going!" No matter what the situation, we always managed to have a few laughs together.

A particularly moving moment occurred after the competition ended. The winners and the jury were invited to Jerusalem, where the winners played a concert. The first prize that year went to a young German by the name of Gerhard Oppitz, who is now having a very fine career. At the concert in Jerusalem, Oppitz played Beethoven's Emperor Concerto. Later, at a reception at the residence of the president of Israel, Mr. Oppitz was asked to say a few words. In a very beautiful speech he declared that he never would have believed that a German pianist could one day win first prize in Israel after what Germany did to the Jewish people. I was very touched by what he said.

Many times I have been asked which pianist playing today I particularly like. Actually, I have heard many promising young artists, and my own former student, Lambert Orkis, who came to study with me after he heard my Chopin, is one of the very best. He's a great talent making a tremendous career for himself, especially as the accompanist for violinist Sophie Anne Mutter and, before that, for cellist Mstislav Rostropovich. I am very happy for Lambert.

I have also heard many not-so-promising pianists who are all technique and no soul. Some just bang the hell out of the piano, and one is worth a story. One evening in São Paulo, Brazil, I went with Sarah, my former wife, to a concert in a museum, and a pianist from Argentina, I believe, came out and played very nicely during the first half of the program. At the end of intermission the lights went out, and everyone waited for the pianist to return to the stage. All of a sudden he came running in from the outer hallway, and as he charged up the aisle, he shook people by their shoulders and shouted, "Get up! Get up!" Finally someone finally said to him, "Hey, what do you think you're doing?" I said to Sarah, "If he comes to you and shakes you like that, I'm going to punch him in the mouth. I really will!" I would not have hurt his hands but just punched him in the mouth.

He created a tremendous amount of tension in the hall and then went up on the stage. During the intermission an old, small grand piano had been brought out. He went over to it and hit its keys with his two fists. Then he picked up an ax that had been placed on stage and proceeded to demolish the piano!

Later that night we went to his reception and met the man. I said to him, "You played very nicely in the first half: what happened in the second half? Were you bitten by a dog or something?"

"Oh, no. I just played the music the way it was written."

"What music?" I said. "You call that music? Who wrote it, some guy in a nuthouse?" Anything to get attention and publicity. That's the quick, easy way to create a sensation, but making an impression with playing skill and musical talent—that's the harder way.

When it comes to today's composers, I take my cue from Mr. Gieseking. He often played new works, but his great program was Bach, Mozart, Beethoven, Brahms, Schubert, Schumann, Debussy, Ravel, and some Chopin and Liszt. He realized that the public generally has little interest in new works. Mr. Gieseking used to say that people who pay for tickets don't want to have to listen to something that they don't know. He said that ticket buyers shouldn't have to ask, "What are they playing, modern music or wrong notes?"

Return to Warsaw

For me Warsaw is and always will be a living cemetery where the world I once knew and loved is no more, but where the ghosts from that world are everywhere. In October 1992 I got the opportunity to return to Warsaw when Kazimierz Kord, the conductor of the Warsaw Philharmonic, invited me to perform Chopin's E Minor Piano Concerto with the orchestra. My friend and student, Dr. Gregg Pressman, accompanied me a third of a century—thirty-three years—after my previous visit.

Although the city was very different from what it had been before the war, so much so that I sometimes wondered if I had ever really lived there, my return to Warsaw brought back a flood of memories. Unlike my visit in 1959, which took place during the height of the Cold War, the atmosphere on this visit was very different. This time I could go freely around the city with open eyes and an open heart.

The destruction of Old Warsaw had begun with the German invasion in 1939 and the razing of the Jewish Ghetto in 1943, but it was the systematic demolition of the city after the Germans crushed

217

the Polish uprising in 1944 that left the city 85 percent destroyed. The Germans burned and dynamited buildings on a massive scale to teach the Poles a lesson. Although many historic buildings were reconstructed after the war—the government rebuilt the medieval castle and painstakingly restored the Old City on the river to its fifteenth-century appearance—the city bore little resemblance to what it once had been. Monuments and plaques were everywhere, including a monument to the Warsaw Ghetto Uprising about 150 feet from where I was born. The whole Jewish part of the city does not exist any more. There are different buildings and a different layout of streets. Before Hitler the Jewish district was an extremely busy neighborhood, but now it's all quiet, peaceful, empty.

Driving on Sienna Street, I spotted the house where I had seen my mother and my father and my sister Helen together for the last time. It's a dilapidated relic now, but there were once marble floors and an elevator for its seven or eight stories. It had contained my uncle's apartment, where we lived after my uncle fled with his wife and children to Bialystok. We stopped the car, and we went in and looked around. I paused in front of one of the doors and said, "This has to be the one." When I knocked, a big dog barked. Everything else was quiet. It was noontime. The occupants were probably at work, so we couldn't get in. Farther down the street at Sienna 30, the building where my brother Joel had lived with his wife was gone.

I played my concert with the Warsaw Philharmonic on a piano that was so heavy I was ready to give up and go home. You had to jump on the keys to play it. It was typical of German-made Steinways, which were so heavy, it's a joke—unless you have to play them. "It's a brand new Steinway from Hamburg," I was told. Well, I could see that it was new and beautiful, but you couldn't *play* it. The weight of the keys was murder. It had barely been broken in yet. I physically could not play my concerto on that piano at the speed that I normally play it. I was ready to quit, but then I just decided that I'd play the first and third movements slower than I normally do, and it worked out. However, when I went on to Copenhagen and played on a beautiful light piano, I taped the concertos and sent the recording to the conductor in Warsaw. I wrote, "This is what I sound like when I play on a normal piano!" When it comes to pianos, however, *normal* is a relative term—unfortunately.

While in Warsaw I made several pilgrimages. I went to Holy Christ Church, where Chopin's heart is buried in a vault in one of the pillars. I also visited the house where Chopin was born outside the city of Zelazowa Wola. As Gregg and I were standing outside, I heard a group speaking German, so I went over and asked them where they were from and if they were musicians.

"We are pianists from Darmstadt. Are you a pianist, too?"

"Yes."

"You speak such good German. Did you study in Germany?"

"Yes, I did."

"Who was your teacher?"

When I said Walter Gieseking, they were all in raptures.

I had a two-hour interview on the Polish State Radio with the director of the music department, Jan Popis. I also telephoned Kazimierz Wilkomirski, who had been the conductor of the Warsaw Philharmonic back in 1930 when I played the Mozart concerto for the Philharmonic for the second time at age twelve. By now Wilkomirski was in his late nineties and could barely speak. When I mentioned that I had played with him more than sixty years earlier, he said in a frail, high voice, "I don't remember."

I also went to Majdanek. Gregg insisted that we make the trip. I needed to be persuaded because, frankly, I felt trepidation at the thought of returning. When I saw what was left of the camp, I was amazed by how many feelings and memories flooded back, especially after seeing barrack 16 again after almost half a century. Barrack 16, the barrack surrounded by a fence where they put the survivors of the Warsaw Ghetto Uprising. Barrack 16, where we received "special treatment," where they woke us up with a club and whoever didn't get up off the bunk right away was killed instantly. Barrack 16, where after a few weeks I was so weak I couldn't make it up the small step without holding onto the door handle and pulling myself up. It was one of the many hundreds of other barracks. We took photos—not that I'll ever forget what Majdanek looked like. It was luck, pure luck, that I survived that hell and am alive to tell about it.

Today at the camp stands a memorial in three languages—Russian on top, English in the middle, and German below. The English translation reads:

Prisoners brought to the Majdanek camp represented 51 nationalities from the following 26 countries: Albania, Austria, Belgium, Bulgaria, China, Czechoslovakia, Denmark, Finland, France, Germany, Great Britain, Greece, Holland, Hungary, Italy, Luxembourg, Norway, Poland, Rumania, the Soviet Union, Spain, Sweden, Switzerland, Turkey, the United States of America, Yugoslavia. Poles, Jews and Soviet people were most numerously represented. The prisoners belonged to a variety of social and professional groups. They were differentiated also in terms of age, education, cultural background and moral level. Prisoners were transported in inhuman conditions. After arrival at the camp they were sorted out. Those unfit for labour were usually sent into gas chambers, while those judged fit for staying in the camp were registered and dressed into striped clothing. Each prisoner was given a number replacing his name and labelled with a triangular emblem whose colour denoted the reason for being held in the camp.

There are still containers of gas at Majdanek, horrible reminders of what happened there. Small innocent-looking metal containers that murdered hundreds of thousands. The ovens are still there, too.

The earth at Majdanek is soft now, but when I was imprisoned there, it was hard as stone. The fields, fed with the blood of the thousands murdered and buried there, has grown verdant. As Gregg and I walked through the camp, it felt to me as if we were walking on dead bodies.

In Warsaw we also visited what had once been the *Umschlagplatz*, the area at the edge of the former Warsaw Ghetto where the Germans murdered hundreds of people every day while they transported thousands more to Nazi death camps. It's strange to hear how quiet it is there now. You would think you would still be able to hear the screams and the rifle shots and the moans of the dying and still smell the fear, but you can't—at least not during the day.

The big elementary school, built near the *Umschlagplatz* shortly before the war, was still there. The Germans had used it to hold people overnight before transporting them to their deaths. I spent the night in its basement with my mother, my sister, and my brother Joel and his wife. It has since become a school again, so I visited it. I went in and spoke perfect Polish so they wouldn't know anything. "I was here many years ago," I said, "and I'd like to go down to the basement and see what it looks like now." "Oh, sure," they said, "go ahead."

The basement is now nothing but a cloakroom—just lots of coats hanging there. You would never have known anything happened there or the hell that people went through in that place. I don't know what I expected to find or see. Maybe ghosts. But certainly not just coats.

Sometimes when I'm asked how I managed to survive all the horrors of the camps, I have a very simple answer: I was extremely lucky many, many times. There were so many miracles, it was unreal. So many lucky breaks. I must have had an angel sitting on my shoulder or hiding in my pocket. Some of my friends insist that my wonderful mother continued to watch over me. That I don't know. I'd like to think so.

Since I witnessed the selection process firsthand, I know that usually it came down to the fact that I was young, I was strong, and the Germans needed able bodies to do their work. I was set aside, selected, and *allowed* to live, at least for the time being, because they found me useful. It had nothing to do with who or what I was or could be. To them I was just a pair of hands to help their Machine, pure and simple. I was of use, and if I hadn't been, I wouldn't be here.

Of all the people who were of no use to them, God, what can

I say? I knew so many who perished—special, incredibly talented individuals. Just in my immediate family. My father, Adam, was a brilliant businessman who remained strong even in his sixties. I remember once when I was still just a kid watching him dive off a high diving platform and thinking he was going to kill himself. When I started crying, he told me, "Stop crying and just keep watching!" And then he made the most beautiful dive I've ever seen. Everybody who was there to see it applauded.

He had extraordinary courage. After the Nazis seized his clothing business, he returned for money he had hidden away in one of the bolts of cloth so he could buy food for his family. Even though he was seventy years old at the time, he entered, grabbed the bolt from right under their noses, and ran off zigzagging with bullets flying around him and soldiers shouting "Halt!" He took this incredible risk to feed his hungry family.

My brother Ignaz was a brilliant engineer who could play piano totally by ear. He would go to a show and come home and sit down and play all the tunes he had heard. He was also gifted with perfect pitch. And funny too. He used to make up incredible jokes for us all the time. We would sneak into his room late at night and gather around his bed, and he'd say, "I've got some new jokes for you," and he would send us all into gales of laughter and get us into trouble, my father yelling from his bedroom, "You boys cut it out and go to bed!"

And my sister Helen. She was so beautiful, absolutely beautiful, so exquisite, like a mimosa, a delicate flower, with a voice like an angel. She used to help me with my schoolwork, and she helped teach me to play the piano, and then when I began to learn, I began to teach her. The sweetest person in the world.

And my wonderful, incomparable mother, Esther, with the most beautiful smile—when she smiled, you saw heaven.

I still remember all of them, hold them close in my heart, and I kiss their photographs last thing at night and first thing in the morning.

It is fitting that I conclude my memoir with the *Umschlagplatz*, the last place where I saw my dear mother, my sister Helen, and my sister-in-law Ala. I will never forget it. It was on the morning of Monday, January 18, 1943—the morning of the German assault on the ghetto, which they called *Aktion II*. The SS had surrounded Mila 7, where the Germans kept their Jewish railroad workers and what was left of their families. The Nazis were going from window to window trying to see if people were inside. When they saw birds gathering outside one of the windows, they figured that people must be hiding. We were in there all right, and now it was to be our turn to be rounded up.

It took until about 3:30 in the afternoon before the Germans discovered us. There were maybe thirty people in hiding in the room where we lived. I was there with my mother, my sister, my brother Joel, and his wife. They took us all out and marched us along Za-menhof Street through the burning ghetto all the way to the *Um-schlagplatz*, with the SS walking us the whole way with their guns pointed at us. Nobody among us had even half a weapon. They marched us through that horror, that hell, through all the smoke and fire.

They put us in the basement of the new elementary school next to the *Umschlagplatz* for the night. A Polish policeman on guard on the back side of the building—I could look up through the base-ment window and tell from his shoes and trousers that he was a policeman—was marching back and forth. I called up to try to talk to him. I said, "Officer, come over here, I want to tell you some-thing."

"Shut up," he said. "They're going to make soap out of you!" That was his answer.

The next morning, when they ordered us outside, I ended up standing next to a young girl, probably around eighteen, who worked at a Luftwaffe camp that used Jewish workers. When this girl saw her chief, her *meister*, looking around for his workers, she called out to him, "Meister, Meister, I'm over here."

A German SS man pulled out his gun, took aim, and killed her with one shot to the head. Just like that. She was standing about a yard from me. At first I thought he might be aiming at me. He killed that beautiful girl. I'll never forget it. Then he calmly turned back to the conversation he was having with another German like a perfect gentleman, acting as if he had just smoked a cigarette or something. You would never believe he had just murdered someone.

After the German railway people figured out where we were when we didn't show up for work, they came to the *Umschlagplatz* and demanded that the SS give us back. "You want to keep the trains rolling to the front, don't you? How are we supposed to do it without the Jews?"

So the SS commander said, "Okay, we'll let you have the men, but the women we'll keep here until tomorrow." That was a lie, a big lie.

When they told us that the men were to return to work but they were keeping the women, I held onto my mother and didn't want to leave her. My brother Joel pulled me, saying, "Come on, come on. We have to go. They'll release them tomorrow." My mother said, "Go, go. I bless you. You'll survive this horror. You'll become a great pianist, and I'll be very proud of you." Those were the last words I ever heard from my mother. I shall never forget them.

Later after work, when Joel and I came back to look for them, they were gone. I don't know for certain where they killed my mother. I never will. Most likely they murdered her at Treblinka, because that's where the trains were headed in those days.

Index